**SUCCESS
CAN
BE
YOURS**

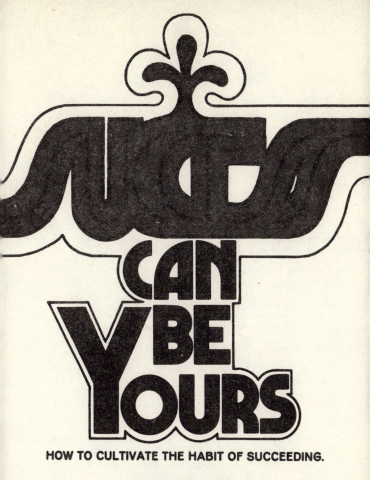

SUCCESS CAN BE YOURS

HOW TO CULTIVATE THE HABIT OF SUCCEEDING.

Mack R. Douglas

ZONDERVAN PUBLISHING HOUSE

OF THE ZONDERVAN CORPORATION
GRAND RAPIDS, MICHIGAN 49506

Success Can Be Yours
Formerly published as
How to Cultivate the Habit of Succeeding
Copyright © 1968 by Zondervan Publishing House
Grand Rapids, Michigan

Library of Congress Catalog Card Number 68-10520

Seventh printing 1977
ISBN 0-310-23872-2

ACKNOWLEDGMENTS

To Walt Dunn and station WFLT, Fort Lauderdale,
who presented this book over the period of a year each
afternoon at 4:30, five days a week.

To Nell Seaver and Mary Evelyn Jaquess for manuscript production.

Printed in the United States of America

DEDICATION

As a salesman, while still in his early twenties, he became the sales leader in the nation's largest exclusive weekly premium life insurance company.

As a Sales Manager he built a sales organization of eight hundred men in twenty-four months that produced thirty million dollars of intangible sales. Before he was twenty-seven, in sales and sales management his personal work had reached more than one million dollars. His personal earnings had averaged more than $100,000 per year for more than a decade.

In 1960 he founded Success Motivation Institute in Waco, Texas, a firm dedicated to motivating people to their full potential.

This book is dedicated to a man that only America can produce, an outstanding example of the principles of personal achievement — Paul J. Meyer.

FOREWORD

Until comparatively recent times, the word "habit" had a negative connotation. It was inexorably linked with something we should not do. We were urged to develop good rules or customs of behavior, not habits.

Now we know that the principal function of human thought is to produce habits of action. We can develop good habits just as easily as bad ones. Furthermore, the habit that results from our thinking depends upon how it causes us to act. And, as Mr. Douglas so convincingly proves in the following pages, we can even cultivate the habit of succeeding.

It is a sad and regrettable fact that most human beings go through their lives wholly unaware that personal success depends on how they think and act, not on heredity or environment.

Discovering the full range of his own potential abilities; a determined effort to develop the habit of succeeding, is not something an intelligent person leaves to the chances of life. It is something he pursues systematically to the end of his days. In my opinion, this book makes an invaluable contribution to that pursuit.

Paul J. Meyer, President
Success Motivation ® Institute, Inc.
Waco, Texas

ACKNOWLEDGMENTS

Gratitude is expressed to the following for permission to quote from their copyrighted materials:

Appleton-Century-Crofts for the quotes taken from *Leaders and Leadership* by Emory S. Bogardus.

Bobbs-Merrill Co., Inc. for the quotes taken from *How Never to Be Tired* by Marie Beynon Rey.

Charles Scribner's Sons for quote taken from *Types of Philosophy* by William Hocking.

Doubleday & Co., Inc. for the quotes taken from *How to Strengthen Your Will Power* by Frank Kingdom and from *How to Live on Twenty-four Hours a Day* by Arnold Bennett.

Fawcett Publishing Co. for the quote taken from *The Master Key to Riches* by Napoleon Hill.

Fleming H. Revell Co. for the quote taken from *How I Discovered the Secret of Success in the Bible* by Clint Davidson.

Follett Publishing Co. for the quote taken from *Don't Be Afraid* by Edward Cowles.

Harper & Row Publishers, Inc., for the quote taken from *Your Key to Creative Thinking* by Samm S. Baker.

Harvard University Press for the quote taken from an article by D. W. Ewing in the September, 1964 issue of the "Harvard Business Review."

Lincoln Electric Company for the quote taken from *Incentive Management* by James F. Lincoln.

Macfadden, Bartell Corp. (Harper & Row) for the quote taken from *Man, the Unknown* by Dr. Alexis Carel.

Macmillan Company (Crowell Collier, Inc.) for the quotes from *Why People Work* by Aaron Levenstein.

McGraw-Hill Book Company for the quotes taken from *Tired Feelings and How to Master Them* by Donald A. and Eleanor C. Laird.

Napoleon Hill Foundation for the quotes taken from *How to Sell Your Way Through Life* by Ralston and *The Law of Success* by Ralston.

National Council of Churches of Christ for permission to quote from the Revised Standard Version of the Bible, copyright © 1946 and 1952 by the Division of Christian Education of the National Council of Churches of Christ.

New American Library, Inc. for the quotes taken from *The Eloquence of Winston Churchill* by F. B. Czarnomski.

Simon and **Schuster, Inc.** for the quotes taken from *Peace of Mind* by Joshua Liebman, from *Release From Nervous Tension* by Harold Fink and from *The Dale Carnegie Scrapbook* by Dorothy Carnegie.

Prentice-Hall Inc. for the quotes taken from the following books:

TNT, The Power Within You, by Claude Bristol and Harold Sherman

The Success System That Never Fails by Clement Stone

Grow Rich While You Sleep by Ben Sweetland

All the Time You Need by Robert Updegraff

Magic of Believing by Claude Bristol

The Power of the Subconscious Mind by Joseph Murphy

How I Multiplied My Income and Happiness in Selling by Frank Bettger

How I Raised Myself from Failure to Success in Selling by Frank Bettger

Successful Leadership in Business by Charles Cerami

How to Live 365 Days a Year by John A. Schindler

Master Your Tensions and Enjoy Living by H. Milt and G. Stevenson

Action Power by Vernon Howard

The Knack of Using Your Subconscious Mind by J. K. Williams

How to Sell Yourself to Others by Elmer Wheeler

The Magic Power of Self-Image Psychology by Maxwell Maltz

Van Nostrand Co. for the quote taken from *The Anti-Capitalistic Mentality* by Ludwig von Mises.

Wehman Brothers for the quote taken from *The Power of Concentration* by Theron Q. Dumont.

CONTENTS

SUCCESS
CAN
BE
YOURS

1.

THE POWER OF THE WILL

Dr. Russell H. Conwell once said, "There has been altogether too much talk about the secret of success. Success has no secret. Her voice is forever ringing through the market place and crying in the wilderness, and the burden of her cry is one word — will. Any man who hears and heeds that cry is equipped fully to climb to the very heights of life. If there is one thing I've tried to do through these years it is to indent in the minds of the men of America the living fact that when they give Will the reins and say, 'Drive,' they are headed toward the heights."[1]

Meet King Will

The will is the master of the world. All emotions fall like slaves at the feet of King Will. Did you know that the gray matter of our minds is plastic and can be fashioned according to our will? The only thing in the world that you and I totally control is our mind. Will is master of the mind. The

[1]Haddock, Frank, *Power of the Will* (Cleveland: Ralston Publishing Co., 1948).

moment King Will decides and initiates the accomplishment of his purpose through decisive action all emotions and mind power immediately fall into disciplined lines of military drill, ready for immediate orders to accomplish the commands of King Will.

The annals of history tell us that men who formerly were slaves and who have come to power themselves tend to be dictators, to control the minds, emotions and wills of others just as they themselves were formerly controlled. This is true when such men have not mastered their wills but have let their wills master them.

The greatest danger to a democratic society is that many individuals are given more freedom than they can imagine. Individual discipline is the basis of any free society and men cannot remain free unless through their will power they choose right over wrong, freedom over slavery, and justice to others over injustice and tyranny.

In a recent survey in the United States it was found that 96% of the people interviewed believed in God. However, 72% of these people indicated that their belief in God had nothing to do with their ethical behavior — that they could do as they pleased. This is a tragic danger signal, warning us that men have not disciplined their wills to follow the dictates of their beliefs. In religious circles such individuals are called hypocrites who profess one thing and practice another.

Three Kinds of People

There are three kinds of individuals: (1) The psychologically dependent person who goes along with the crowd. This group makes up the vast majority of our population, sheep without a shepherd, a mob without a master. These are men without wills, wanderers. (2) The psychologically independent person or the rebel who is hostile to all other individuals and control. This individual starts a new movement but is so psychologically undeveloped that when others join his movement he soon will leave it and start another. (3) The independent thinker who remains true to his convictions regardless of what anyone else says or does or thinks. This individual has mastered King Will. He wants to go with the crowd but will take his stand whether anyone else stands with him or not. He is the Abraham Lincoln of his day; the General Douglas MacArthur; the bold champion of truth.

Epictetus once said, "There is nothing good or evil save in the will." And Goethe said, "He who is firm in will molds the world to himself." Confucius has said, "You can capture the Commander-in-chief of three armies, but you cannot overcome a private man's will." And Epictetus again said, "Ask not that events should happen as you will, but let your will be that events should happen as they do, and you shall have peace." Novalis said, "Character is a perfectly educated will." And William Law said, "The will is that which has all power; it makes heaven and it makes hell; for there is no hell but where the will of the creature is turned from God, nor any heaven but where the will of the creature worketh with God."

Will is the power of self-direction. It may be called the faculty of conscious, or the activity of deliberate action. The will is not feeling, for one can feel without willing and one can will contrary to feeling. Royce has said, "By the term will in the narrower sense one very commonly means so much of our mental life as involves the attentive guidance of our conduct. Will is commonly called volition. A volition is the willing power in action."

In his book, *The Power of the Will*,[2] Frank Haddock says that will power is: First, mental capacity for single volitional act. It is the mind's ability to throw great energy into a given command for action by itself or by other beings.

[2]*Ibid.*

Emerson calls it, "The spasm to collect and swing the whole man." Secondly, the will is not only a dynamic force in mind, it is also a power of persistent adherence to a purpose. For example, the will may exhibit enormous energy in isolated instances while being utterly weak with reference to a continuous course of conduct or for any general purpose in life. The will is to choose in order to act. The person chooses; but in a general way the will may be defined now as a power to choose what the man shall do. Then through volition there follows the ideal action.

Four Steps to Will Power

Haddock suggests four steps with the act of willing: (1) Presentation in mind of something that may be done. (2) Presentation in mind of motives or reasons relating to what may be done. (3) The rise in mind of sufficient reasons. (4) Putting forth in mind a volition corresponding to sufficient reason.

A great Chinese proverb says: "Great souls have wills; feeble ones have only wishes." And Gratian said, "At twenty years of age the will reigns; at thirty, the wit; and at forty, the judgment." Tryon Edwards has said, "The highest obedience in the spiritual life is to be able always and in all things to say, 'Not my will but thine be done.'" Seneca said, "No action will be considered bravery unless the will was so, for by the will the act was dictated." Epictetus once said, "In the schools of the wrestling master, when a boy falls he is bidden to get up again and to go on wrestling day by day until he has acquired strength; and we must do the same and not after one failure suffer ourselves to be swept along as by a torrent. You need but will, and it is done; but if you relax your efforts you will be ruined; for ruin and recovery are both from within." Shakespeare once said, "The will of man is by his reason swayed." And Colton said, "To commit the execution of a purpose to one who disapproves of the plan of it is to employ but one third of the man; his heart and his head against you, for you have commanded only his hands." South stated, "Whatever the will commands, the whole man must do; the empower of the will over all the faculties being absolutely overruling and despotic." And W. Humboldt has said, "In the moral world there is nothing impossible if we can bring a thorough will to do it. Man can do everything with himself, but he must not attempt to do too much with others."

It was Lavater who said, "Calmness of will is a sign of grandeur. The vulgar, far from hiding their will blab their wishes. A single spark of occasion discharges the child of passion into a thousand crackers of desire." Montaigne has said, "We cannot be held to what is beyond our strength and means; for at times the accomplishment and execution may not be in our power, and indeed there is nothing really in our own power except the will: on this are necessarily based and founded all the principles that relegate the duty of man." And Schiller said, "Every man stamps his value on himself. The price we challenge for ourselves is given us by others. Man is made great or little by his own will."

From Victor Hugo we have, "People do not lack strength; they lack will." And Milton has said, "If the will which is the law of our nature were withdrawn from our memory, fancy, understanding, and reason, no other hell for a spiritual being could equal what we should then feel from the anarchy of our power. It would be conscious madness, a horrid thought." And Froude once said, "To deny the freedom of the will is to make morality impossible."

Emerson said, "There can be no driving force, except through the conversion of the man into his will, making him the will and the will him."

Now the big question is, "Who is your king?" If you have made emotion and the sensate mind your master you are a fickle slave of any and every feeling or sensual desire that confronts you on your journey of life. If you let King Mind master you, you may find yourself chained to your library, worshiping intellectuality and a hermit, isolated from all practicality. But if you have made Will King, your action will propel you into life's battles with the disciplined slaves of emotional feeling and mental training, helping you to storm the fortresses of achievement. Make Will your King. You can make a habit of succeeding.

Power of the Will

Claude Bristol and Harold Sherman in their book, *TNT, The Power Within You,* say, "People who claim they have never been able to make their higher powers of mind work for them have, on the contrary, through wrong thinking, forced these very powers to work against them. They have caused these powers to produce failure instead of success, misery instead of happiness."[3] It is commonly believed among business circles that pessimistic thinking and talk can actually lead this nation into a depression by simply constantly emphasizing the problems of this nation.

Remember the positive, dynamic words of President Franklin Delano Roosevelt when he said, "The only thing we have to fear is fear itself." In the Bible Job said, "For the thing which I greatly feared is come upon me, and that which I was afraid of is come unto me" (Job 3:25). And the power of the will can drive out all worry, despondency, discouragement, pessimism and every other foul and vicious emotion. Will power is expressed with such strong words as explosive, decisive, dynamic, impelling, restraining, deliberative, persistent, powerful and assertive. The strong will is master of the man, controlling and directing the body according to the dictates of desire or reason.

[3]Bristol, Claude and Sherman, Harold, *TNT, the Power Within You* (Englewood Cliffs, N. J.: Prentice-Hall, Inc., 1954).

Haddock tells the story of James Tyson, a bushman in Australia, who died with a fortune of $25,000,000.00.[4] "But," Tyson said, "Money is nothing. It was the little game that was fun." Being asked, "What was the little game?" he replied with amazing energy of concentration, "Fighting the desert. That has been my work. I've been fighting the desert all my life, and I have won. I have put water where there is no water, and beef where there is no beef. I have put fences where there were no fences, and roads where there were no roads. Nothing can undo what I have done, and millions will be happier for it after I am long dead and forgotten." What a dynamic demonstration of will power. And Fowell Buxton said, "The longer I live the more certain I am that the great difference between men, between the feeble and the powerful, the great and the insignificant, is energy — invincible determination — a purpose once fixed, and then death or victory. That quality will do anything that can be done in this world; and no talents, no circumstances, no opportunities will make a two-legged creature a man without it."

Ik Marvel said, "Resolve is what makes a man manifest; not puny resolves, not crude determinations, not errant purpose — but that strong and indefatigable will which treads down difficulties and danger, as a boy treads down the heaving frost lands of winter; which kindle his eye and brain with a proud pulsebeat toward the unattainable. Will makes men giants."

Will Power Made Them Great

Let me give you some demonstrations of the power of will. William Pitt was born with a definite aim in life. From a child he was made to realize that a great career was expected of him, worthy of his renowned father. This was the keynote of all of his instruction.

---

[4]Haddock, *Ibid*.

Abraham Lincoln, in speaking of the power of Ulysses S. Grant, said, "The great thing about him is true persistency of purpose. He is not easily excited, and he has got the grip of a bulldog. When he once gets his teeth in, nothing can shake him off." Remember his words, "I will fight on this line if it takes all summer."

As a small boy General Douglas MacArthur was taught by the forcefulness of his brilliantly decorated father and by the dynamics of his mother that he had a date with destiny. In World War I he exposed himself time after time, somehow with an inner conviction that it wasn't his date to die. Men of lesser convictions called it egomania when he said to the Filipino people, "I will return." The dynamics of that conviction was the pulsebeat of the war of the Pacific. If the parents will it that their children will excel, and will spend the time, the love, the affection, the attention, of a disciplined education of the power of suggestion regarding their destiny those children will arise to heights of outstanding achievement.

One of America's outstanding business leaders is W. Clement Stone, fabulous insurance executive, President of Combined Insurance Company of America, and other insurance companies, editor and publisher of Success Unlimited Magazine, and author of, *The Success System That Never Fails*. Let me quote Clement Stone, "Success can be reduced to a formula and failure can be reduced to a formula too. Apply the one and avoid the other. Think for yourself. . . . Success is achieved by those who try, for there is nothing to lose by trying and a great deal to gain if successful, by all means try. . . . Time is one of the most important ingredients in any successful formula for any human activity. Save time. Invest it wisely. . . . Thinking will not overcome fear, but action will. . . . In the end, your environment will control you; therefore, make sure that you control your environment. Avoid situations, acquaintances, associates, who tend to hold you back."[5]

Remember the words of Andrew Carnegie, "The man who acquires the ability to take full possession of his own mind may take possession of everything else to which he is justly entitled. . . . And the man who masters himself through self-discipline never can be mastered by others."

In his book, *The Master Key to Riches,* Napoleon Hill gives us the ten factors in self-discipline: "(1) Infinite intelligence. (2) The conscious mind. (3) The faculty of will power. (4) The faculty of reason. (5) The faculty of the emotions. (6) The faculty of imagination. (7) The faculty of the conscious. (8) The sixth sense. (9) The memory. (10) The five physical senses."[6]

Will power is the progressive action of strong self-discipline. The power of the will is the totality of all of the powers of human personality yoked, marshaled, and harnessed together to achieve dynamic purpose. You can make a habit of succeeding by depending on the power of your will.

Cultivating Your Will

Professor William James is quoted in the book, *Power of the Will,* "The great thing in all education is to make our nervous system our ally instead of our enemy. For this we must make automatic and habitual, as early as possible, as many useful actions as we can, and as carefully guard against growing into ways that are likely to be disadvantageous. In the acquisition of a new habit, or the leaving off of an old one, we must take care to launch ourselves with as strong and decided intuition as possible.

---

[5]Stone, Clement, *The Success System That Never Fails* (Englewood Cliffs, New Jersey: Prentice-Hall, Inc., 1962).
[6]Hill, Napoleon, *The Master Key to Riches* (Greenwich, Conn.: Fawcett Publications, Inc.).

"Never suffer an exception to occur till the new habit is securely rooted in your life.

"Seize the very first possible opportunity to act on every resolution you make and on every emotional prompting you may experience in the direction of the habit you aspire to gain."[7]

Haddock also gives us the principles in will training: "(1) Any direct effort to cultivate the perceptive powers must affect the growth of memory, imagination and reason. (2) Any direct effort to cultivate the memory must affect the growth of the perceptive powers, imagination and reason. (3) Any direct effort to cultivate the imagination must affect the growth of the perceptive powers of memory and reason. (4) Any direct effort to cultivate the reasoning powers must affect the perceptive powers, memory and imagination. (5) Any direct effort to cultivate the moral faculties must affect the growth of the perceptive powers, memory, imagination and reason. (6) And any direct effort to cultivate the perceptive powers, memory and imagination, reasoning or moral faculties, must affect the growth of the will."[8]

Recently Cliff Hagen, twice all-American on the University of Kentucky basketball team, and for eight years pro-basketball forward with the St. Louis Hawks and a member of the world championship St. Louis Hawks' team of 1957-58, visited us and spoke at a high school basketball banquet and presented a basketball clinic. It was interesting to observe how that this dedicated athlete, the smallest man on the front line in all of the N.B.A., had learned many unique, original, and amazing tactics in order to counteract the superior height of men who were guarding him. Cliff pointed out that it was the discipline of years of training and of intensive desire to excel that led him to achieve.

[7]Haddock, *Ibid.*
[8]*Ibid.*

That's the answer. You must develop your will power by a series of systematic exercises that will cultivate your volitional strength until no one can sway you to chase rabbits when you should be after the birds.

Will Discipline

When John Huss was arrested and told that he was to be burned at the stake for his religion he practiced will power by holding his hand and arm over a flaming fire until he could will the control of his convictions over the demands of the pain of his physical body. He scarred his body for days. He burned himself in preparation.

Now the second way that we develop will power is by the strengthening of the mind through a process of disciplined study. We come to an unquestioned conviction that this is the only course to pursue. Why not spend one hour every day in disciplined mental development? Why throw away these precious hours sitting in front of that little idiot box, gazing at someone else's activity? Get out of the stands and on to the playing field. Become a participant in life's great challenges.

While a student, Billy Graham preached to the cypress stumps in a marshy area near Clearwater, Florida, learning to discipline his voice and to master the principles of preaching. Then in the fall of 1949 in Los Angeles in his first city-wide crusade that gained him international acceptance he was ready; he had disciplined his mind.

William Jennings Bryan had to overcome speech impediments and spend many years preparing himself for his great hour. Before his political party's convention in Chicago he brought his fabulous address, *Crosses of Gold.* That address made him three times nominee for the office of President of the United States. He paid the price of mental discipline.

Eleanor Roosevelt said, "Do what you feel in your heart to be right — for you will be criticized anyway. You will be damned if you do, and damned if you don't." Dale Carnegie said, "Be yourself." Act on the sage advice that Irving Berlin gave the late George Gershwin. When Berlin and Gershwin first met, Berlin was already famous but Gershwin was still a struggling young composer working for $35.00 a week in Tin Pan Alley. Berlin, impressed by Gershwin's ability, offered Gershwin a job as his musical secretary at almost three times the salary he was then getting. "But don't take the job," Berlin advised. "If you do, you may develop into a second-rate Berlin. But if you insist on being yourself, some-day you will become a first-rate Gershwin." And Dale Carnegie said, "If you can hold up your head and admit that you are in the wrong, then a wrong deed can benefit you. For to admit a wrong will not only increase the respect of those about you, it will increase your own self-respect." He also said, "According to the book of Genesis, the Creator gave man dominion over the whole wide earth. A mighty big present. But I'm not interested in any such super-royal prerogatives. All I desire is dominion over myself — and dominion over my thoughts; dominion over my fears; domin-ion over my mind and over my spirit. And the wonderful thing is that I know I can obtain to an astonishing degree, anytime I want to, by merely controlling my actions — which in turn controls my reactions."[9]

Think of Charles Atlas, the 97-pound weakling who be-came so terribly dissatisfied with the way the larger boys would take away his girl friends, so he became the world's best known physical specimen. It has brought him fortune and fame. What an excellent example of will power.

Will Incentive

Will power is incentive. Incentive is that which incites to determination and action.

Earl Nightingale quotes an excellent article from the great

[9]Carnegie, Dorothy, ed., *Dale Carnegie Scrapbook* (New York: Simon and Schuster, 1959).

preacher of another year, Henry Ward Beecher: "If one should give me a dish of sand, and tell me there are particles of iron in it, I might look for them with my eyes, and search for them with my clumsy fingers and be unable to detect them; but let me take a magnet and sweep through it, and it would draw to itself the most invisible particles by the mere power of attraction. The unthankful heart, like my finger in the sand, discovers no mercy; but let the thankful heart sweep through the day, and as the magnet finds the iron, so it will find, in every hour, some heavenly blessing, only the iron in God's sand is gold." That's it. Let your thankful heart sweep through the day and like a magnet it will draw good things to be thankful for. So in cultivating your will power establish first what you want to accomplish, and like a magnet, as you pursue that course without looking to the left or to the right, drawing inspiration from the example of Lot's wife who, looking back, turned into a pillar of salt, and drawing instruction from the words of Jesus when He said, "No man, having put his hand to the plough, and looking back, is fit for the kingdom of God" (Luke 9:62). As you pursue this journey, you will draw the strength from many associations and the wisdom from many contacts to lead you to accomplish your goal.

In his book, *Grow Rich While You Sleep*, Ben Sweetland says, "To develop self-mastery do this: each time a negative thought attempts to enter my mind, I will immediately become aware of it and will dissolve it with a positive thought. My self-confidence is mounting as day by day I gain mastery over self. . . . I am blessed with great powers of mental concentration. I can hold my thoughts on a single idea until I elect to discharge it from my mind. . . . I master my being and can fully relax at will. My mind is dwelling on peaceful, harmonious thoughts."[10] And William Hocking in his book,

[10]Sweetland, Ben, *Grow Rich While You Sleep* (Englewood Cliffs, New Jersey: Prentice-Hall, Inc., 1962).

Types of Philosophy, says, "Psychology has for sometime been critical of that division of mental powers which create intellect, feeling, and will as three distinct and coordinate functions. It has pointed out that feeling, as emotional disturbance, is the beginning of action and submerges with will."[11]

One of the finest things I've ever read on will power is that excellent little booklet, *How to Strengthen Your Will Power,* by Frank Kingdon, published by Nelson Doubleday in, *The Personal Success Program.* He says, "(1) Make sure you want it enough. When you want anything badly enough you will automatically go after it with all that you have. (2) Believe you can do it. Let your past failures have nothing to do with what you are now facing. Furthermore, past failure is no reason for not believing in present success and don't let your pride down. (3) Take one step at a time. You can only think one thought at a time. You can only perform one act at the time. (4) Put yourself on the spot. Tell others what your project is. Write out your goal. (5) Achieve the habit."[12]

Remember, habit reinforces will and self-discipline becomes habit.

Cultivate your will power and you can make a habit of succeeding.

Diseases of the Will

Disease is the want of ease. Dr. Salisbury says, "Mechanical obedience is but one-half the battle; the patient must not only will, he must believe. The whole nature of man must be brought to the task, moral as well as physical, for the seat of the disease is not confined to the body; the vital energies are wasted; the will, often the mind, are impaired. Fidelity

[11]Hocking, William, *Types of Philosophy* (New York: Charles Scribner's Sons, 1960).
[12]Kingdon, Frank, *How to Strengthen Your Will Power* (New York: Doubleday & Co., 1956).

of the body is as nothing if not reinforced by fidelity of the soul. Disease is a destructive action contrary to normal purpose which brings tragic results."[13]

There is no such thing as a weak will. All of us have wills. The will, however, can be surrendered as some do to alcoholism or to dope addiction or to a life of laziness. On the other hand the will may be channeled to outstanding achievement. Where have you channeled your will?

Haddock said, "The diseased condition of the will may result: (1) From a diseased mind, (2) from an ill-developed mind, (3) from causes resident in the will considered as a faculty of the mind. A disease of the will is a disease of the self inasmuch as it is the self that wills."[14] A mind is diseased if there is insanity or depression or worry or fear or other such destructive emotion.

An ill-developed mind is paralysis of decision.

There are four indications of a diseased will. Here they are: (1) The person who does not even admit there is a problem when the problem occurs. The individual who simply shrugs his shoulders and fails to face the reality of responsibility of decision. (2) The person who runs away from the problem, who drops everything and flees in fear. These individuals frequently try to drown their problems in alcohol. However, the problem is still with them, and from a hangover or a dissipated diseased mind it is far worse. (3) The individual who will criticize the conditions that brought about the situation — rather than deciding, this individual blames everybody else. (4) The one who waits for someone else to solve the problem. This is the follower but today we need more leaders.

For example, when you are with a group in a restaurant and each receives the menu, the leader looks it over, may discuss what is offered, may even comment with the waitress

[13]*Power of the Will.*
[14]*Op. cit.*

on what's special. However, the leader decides what he wants and acts. The diseased will waits and takes suggestion from the other, never daring to act for himself. You see, there is a problem — a problem of action and a problem to decide. Such individuals are afraid that the crowd will not agree or that someone will criticize or comment on what they've ordered; or they are afraid it will be too expensive; or they are afraid they will make the wrong decision and get something they will not want; or they are afraid the restaurant will be out of it. It is simply a diseased will — a will that is not excited, dynamic and decisive.

"The saddest failures in life are those that come from not putting forth the power and the will to succeed," said E. P. Whipple. And Confucius said, "The general of a large army may be defeated, but you cannot defeat the determined mind of a peasant." Crabbe once said, "In idle wishes fools supinely stay; be there a will and wisdom finds a way." Nathaniel Hawthorne has said, "Insincerity in a man's own heart must make all his enjoyment, all that concerns him, unreal; so that his whole life must seem like a myriad dramatic representation."

Seize Your Will

Overcome diseases of the mind through dynamic, bold action. Seize your will. Thomas A. Edison said, "If we did all the things we are capable of doing we would literally astound ourselves." Maurice Maeterlinck said, "To look fearlessly upon life; to accept the laws of nature, not with meek resignation, but as her sons, who dare to search and question; to have peace and confidence with our souls — these are the beliefs that make for happiness." And Dale Carnegie has said, "The next time you are tempted to run to someone else to get you out of trouble, say to yourself, 'I can solve this problem myself. If I try to dodge, I'm only fooling myself. I will solve it.' Then go ahead and solve it.

Then you've set your feet upon the path of success."[15]

Many years ago William James said, "Compared to what we ought to be, we are making use of only a small part of our physical and mental resources. Stating the thing broadly, the human individual that lives far within his limits possesses powers of various sorts which he habitually fails to use."[16] Ralph Waldo Emerson gave the perfect antidote to the diseases of the will when he said, "Do not be too timid and squeamish about your actions. All life is an experiment. The more experiments you make the better. What if they are a little coarse, and you may get your coat soiled or torn? What if you do fail, and get fairly rolled in the dirt once or twice? Up again, you shall never be so afraid of a tumble." And Sir Arthur Helps said, "To hear always, to think always, to learn always, it is thus that we live truly; he who aspires to nothing, and learns nothing, is not worthy of living."

You can make a habit of succeeding by mastering your will power by overcoming these diseases of the will.

Success Awaits Your Will

Ralph Waldo Emerson said, "Life is a search after power; and this is an element with which the world is so saturated — that no earnest seeker goes unrewarded." And Dr. Fritz Kunkel says, "Immense hidden powers seem to lurk in the unconscious depth of even the most common man — indeed, of all people without exception it is these powers that are responsible for all great creative effort, whether in the form of a new technical invention or a work of art." It was William Hazlitt who said, "There is nothing more to be esteemed than a manly firmness and decision of character. I like a person who knows his own mind and sticks to it; who sees at once what is to be done in any given circumstances and does it."

---

[15]Carnegie, *Ibid.*
[16]Haddock, *Ibid.*

Emerson said, "A good intention clothes itself with sudden power." And W. M. Paxton said, "Ideas go booming through the world louder than cannons. Thoughts are mightier than armies. Principles have achieved more victories than horsemen and chariots." Centuries ago Garibaldi said, "A bold onset is half the battle." And La Rochefoucauld said, "It is praise-worthy even to attempt a great action." Simms said, "The conditions of conquest are always easy. We have but to toil awhile, endure awhile, believe always, and never turn back."

The only thing in this world that you totally control is your own mind. You can control your mind and your will and success awaits your action. But you cannot wait; you must act now. If you twist a young sapling a crooked tree will tell of the act for centuries to come. Every imprint we make on our wills is expressed in the ages to follow. Always be decisive. Get all the facts. Gather all the information and then act. Make your will master.

Goal Power

You must have a great and challenging goal that will motivate you to give of your best. Then your will must arouse all of your resources to work progressively and aggressively to achieve that goal. But remember, goals are simply check-up points on the way to the dream of purpose. The journey is far more exciting than arriving, and success is yours the minute your will marshalls all of your forces to achieve the goal.

Arthur Brisbane, outstanding newspaper writer and editor, wrote, "The biggest question in life is this: Is it possible to control the will and through the will control oneself in life conditioned?" And then he wrote, "It is possible, in spite of the teachings of superstition, of fatalism, and of mental weakness." William Lecky said, "The discipline of thought is the establishment of an ascendancy of the will over our courses of thinking. The power of casting away morbid trains of reflection and turning resolutely to other subjects or aspects of life; the power of concentrating the mind vigorously on a serious subject and pursuing continuous trains of thought — form perhaps the best fruits of judicious self-education." Remember what Tennyson wrote, "Oh, well for him whose will is strong. He suffers, but he will not suffer long."

Oh, yes, there will be obstacles; there will be temporary defeats; there will be temporary losses, but remember, from every such experience we learn a valuable lesson — we've gained an experience that will help us as long as we live. Surely you agree that any fool can profit by his own mistakes, but the smart fellow profits from the mistakes of others. Learn everything you can from other individuals. Difficulties are advantageous experiences.

Unlimited Will Power

William Ellery Channing wrote, "If you will you can rise. No power in society, no hardship in your condition can depress you, keep you down, in knowledge, in power, virtue, influence, but by your own consent." That's the key word — by your own consent. Let no one else control your will. Let no emotion control your will. Make Will King. Epictetus said, "No man is free who is not master of himself." And J. S. Mill wrote, "The only freedom which deserves the name is that of pursuing our own good, in our own way, so long as we do not attempt to deprive others of theirs, to impede their efforts to obtain it."

Joshua Loth Liebman said, "Let us learn how to accept ourselves — to accept the truth that we are capable in some directions and limited in others, that genius is rare, mediocrity is the portion of almost all of us, but that all of us can contribute from the storehouse of our skills to the enjoyment of our common life. Let us accept our emotional frailties, knowing that every person has some phobia lurking within his mind and that the normal person is he who is willing to accept life with its limitations and its opportunities joyfully and courageously."[17]

Pressense said, "My will, and not thine be done, turned paradise into a desert — not my will but thine be done, turned the desert into paradise and made Gethsemane the gate of heaven." Edwards said, "If we make God's will our law then God's promise shall be our support and comfort and we shall find every burden light and every beauty a joy." James Martineau declared, "All the grand agencies which the progress of mankind evolves are the aggregate result of countless wills, each of which, thinking merrily of its own end, and perhaps fully gaining it, is at the same time enlisted by providence in the secret service of the world." Rabbi Gamaliel stated, "Do God's will as if it were thy will, and He will accomplish thy will as if it were His own." And Longfellow said, "To will what God wills is the only science that gives us rest." S. W. Robertson announced, "Let a man begin with an earnest *I ought* and if he perseveres by God's grace he will end in the free blessedness of *I will.* Let him force himself to abound in such acts of duty, and he will, by and by, find them the joyous habit of his goal."

Norman D. Ford, writing in *Pageant Magazine,* suggests eight ways to improve your will power: (1) In concentration. (2) In observation. (3) In memory. (4) In imagination. (5) In reasoning. (6) In initiative. (7) In persistence. (8) In self-control.

Napoleon Hill said, "A good encyclopedia contains most of the known facts of the world, but they are as useless as sand dunes until organized and expressed in terms of action."

[17]Liebman, Joshua, *Peace of Mind* (New York: Simon and Schuster, 1946).

And Hill added, "Anyone can start but only the thorough-bred will finish."[18]

The minute you start one thing and bring all the power of your being to bear upon it you will have mastered your will. You can make a habit of succeeding.

Your Success Checkup

1. There are three kinds of individuals listed on page 14. Which are you?
2. What part did will power have in James Tyson's earning 25 million dollars?
3. Write out the five-point formula on "How to Strengthen Your Will Power."
4. What are the four indications of a diseased will?
5. What is the only thing in this world that you totally control?
6. List the eight ways to improve your will power.

[18]Hill, Napoleon, *The Laws of Success,* "Science of Personal Achievement" (Charleston, South Carolina: Napoleon Hill Foundation).

2.
CONCENTRATION

Your key to Personal Success is Concentration. Napoleon Hill said "Concentration itself is nothing but a matter of control of the attention."

Focus

Results are the only excuse for activity. Russell Conwell in his matchless message, *Acres of Diamonds*, tells of a Persian fascinated with the desire for diamonds. He sold his farm to travel the world searching for this Queen of Jewels. He lost fortune and health, and diamonds were discovered on his former farm. He had concentrated — but in the wrong direction.

Nothing becomes dynamic until it first becomes specific. Concentration is dissipated unless focused. This amazing faculty sprays in shotgun inefficiency until focused in rifle strength and reached.

As the train can generate no great power until closed valves pinpoint the direct force to the drive shaft, so is focus of our mental dynamics essential in generating mental steam.

Dale Carnegie has so well asked, "Are you doing the work you like best? If not, do something about it. You will never achieve real success unless you like what you are doing. Many men who have achieved success have had to try several things before they knew what they wanted to do." Begin with the focus of your ability on your one burning desire.

Andrew Carnegie did and lowered the price of steel from $160.00 a ton to $20.00 a ton — thus making possible the industrial revolution. He said, "Concentration is my motto — first honesty, then industry and then concentration."

Hubbard wrote, "Genius is only the power of making continuous effort. The line between failure and success is so fine that we scarcely know when we pass it. A little more persistence, a little more effort and what seemed hopeless failure may turn to glorious success. There is no failure except in no longer trying. There is no defeat except from within, no really insurmountable barrier save our own inherent weakness of purpose." Can you focus the totality of your mind, energy, emotions and time on one special goal? If not, then you are not ready or able to concentrate.

Theron Q. Dumont in his power-packed book, *The Power of Concentration,* says: "A man may accomplish almost anything today, if he just sets his heart on doing it and lets nothing interfere with his progress. Say I want to, I can, I will. Only the trained mind can focalize to hold a thought before it, until all the faculties shall have time to consider that thought. This is concentration."[1]

Sir Isaac Newton discovered the law of gravity by thinking about it all the time. He had one simple, sincere and visible goal. He reached it. Remember we become what we think about. Order your sub-conscious mind to ceaselessly

[1]Dumont, Theron Q., *The Power of Concentration* (New York: Wehman Brothers Publishers, 1918).

focalize on your purpose. When we concentrate forcefully other related thoughts flow upon us like torrents of the spring thaw.

Chesterfield once said, "The power of applying attention, steady and undissipated, to a single object is the sure mark of a superior genius."

Indecision is the shark that consumes you after millions of minnows have nibbled away your powers of mental alertness. Force yourself to act. Focus your mind on your chief aim.

La Rouchefoucauld: "Few things are improvable in themselves and it is for want of application, rather than of means, that men fail of success."

Willmot: "Attention makes the genius; all learning, all science and skill depend upon it. Newton traced his great discoveries to it. It builds bridges, opens new worlds, heals diseases, carries on the business of the world. Without it taste is useless in the beauties of literature unobserved."

Sir Isaac Newton: "If I have made any improvement in the sciences it is owing more to patient attention than to anything else."

Reid: "If there is anything that can be called genius it consists chiefly in ability to give that attention to a subject which keeps it steady in the mind, till we have surveyed it accurately on all sides."

You can be successful. You must focus your attention. You must master the art of concentration. Your Key is Concentration.

Visualize

"Fix your attention on a given subject until the outline of that subject has been thoroughly impressed upon the 'sensitized plate' of your mind."[2] — Napoleon Hill.

Paul became the greatest Christian that ever lived because he could do this. His one aspiration: "forgetting what lies

[2]Hill, *Ibid.*

behind and straining forward to what lies ahead, I press on toward the goal . . ." (Philippians 3:13, 14 RSV).

Form a mental image of what you desire to achieve. Place yourself in its picture. Experience the emotions of the moment. Bring to bear the use of the five senses. Feel, see, taste, smell, and hear it.

Say it's a new home. Draw all the details in your mind's eye. Ranch? What color roof? Shingles? Good, how many rooms, four bedrooms, three baths, family room and two-car garage? That's two thousand two hundred square feet. Etch on your brain the floor plan. What color? Natural redwood. It must be in Southern California. Then a palm tree, royal? And a coconut, hibiscus and St. Augustine grass. That's you in the yard standing by the Mercedes Benz. Whose Cadillac, your wife's? Can you smell the hibiscus and cut grass, feel the lines of the Mercedes, hear the birds in the trees, gentle hum of the air-conditioner and taste the sweetness of achievement? It's yours the minute you visualize it and remember the joy of the pursuit of earning it may be greater than living in it.

Think about it several times each day. Soon all your powers will be concentrated on its achievement.

Paul Meyer, president of Success Motivation Institute, told me something in St. Louis that proves this truth. "Vividly imagine, sincerely believe, ardently desire, enthusiastically act and it must inevitably come to pass."

William Lyon Phelps: "One of the chief reasons for success in life is the ability to maintain a daily interest in one's work, to have a chronic enthusiasm, to regard each day as important."

There's a sweetness in achievement that is recognition. The world loves a winner. Schwartz in *The Magic of Thinking Big* says "the desire to be important is man's strongest, most compelling non-biological hunger."

Be different, be successful. Earl Nightingale says that only 5% are.

Washington Gladden: "It is better to say 'This one thing I do' than to say 'These forty things I dabble in.'"

Andrew Carnegie: "Put your eggs in one basket and watch that basket."

You can make a joyous game of concentration by rewarding yourself for each achievement. Emerson said, "Work and thou canst not escape the reward; whether thy work be fine or course, planting corn or writing epics, so only it be honest work, done to thine own approbation, it shall earn a reward to the senses as well as the thought. No matter how often defeated you are born to victory. The reward of a thing well done is to have done it."

Why not enjoy your achievement? Andrew Mellon, secretary-treasurer to three presidents, once paid $300,000 for a coke-making plant and in four years it was worth $15,500,-000. In 1929 his dividends were $94,000,000. Yet he was a lonely man who knew nothing about the enjoyment of money and took no pleasure in spending it.

Life is too short and life is too wonderful to be miserable. Reward yourself for every achievement.

Harold W. Dodds echoes this thought. "No, work is not an ethical duty imposed upon us from without by a misguided and outmoded Puritan morality; it is a manifestation of man's deepest desire that the days of his life shall have significance."[3]

Sir Joshua Reynolds said, "Excellence is never granted to man but as the reward of labor. It argues no small strength of mind to persevere in habits of industry without the pleasure of receiving those advances which, like the hand of a clock, whilst they make hourly approaches to their point yet proceed so slowly as to escape observation."

---

[3]*Dale Carnegie's Scrapbook.*

To Concentrate You Must Organize

Opportunity never knocks except to him who has been seeking opportunity. Then he returns the calls. The more persistently he calls on opportunity the more assuredly opportunity will knock.

1. *Plan your work.* Frank Bettger, insurance salesman extraordinary, master motivator, author of four inspirational best sellers, even schedules his haircuts a week in advance. Frank takes Friday afternoon to organize his work the following week. He is a serene, successful and vibrantly dynamic man. He has no frustration that eats out life's joys by chaotic confusion.

Helen Gardner once helped me with wonderful words of wisdom: "The knife of impatience cuts the nerve of influence."

Bogardus writes, "It was Benjamin Franklin who contrived a method for conducting an examination of his moral conduct. Moreover he devised a plan for correcting his faults. John Wesley kept a diary in which he exactly noted the employment of every hour, including the hour of rising, what he read before breakfast, what he read after breakfast, his hours of preaching."[4] George Whitefield, a contemporary of Wesley, was as dynamic, as dedicated, and as able as Wesley. Whitefield left no organization he followed. Millions of Christians call themselves Methodists to this day because John Wesley planned his work.

William Hoppe, Jr., world champion at billiards for many years used the following formula in concentrating.

A. He eliminated hindrances. No tobacco or liquor to achieve perfect nerve control.

B. Concentrated every energy on the game.

C. Every shot he tried to make a perfect shot.

---

[4]Bogardus, Emory S., *Leaders and Leadership* (New York: Appleton-Century-Crofts, 1934).

D. Second ball lie. He shot so as to set up the ball for the next shot.

E. He eternally practiced.

2. *Do the hard job first.* Ernest Hemingway was at his desk at 8:00 every morning and wrote for hours without ceasing.

Schedule your hardest task first and then you are free from the apprehension and fear of a distasteful job ahead. The day gets easier and more joyful. Also you are uplifted knowing that you have been victor rather than victim.

Master your emotions. I once counseled with a fourteen-year-old who had been expelled from school because of his ungovernable temper. Joe agreed with me that we would assign an emotion to his fingers — thumb, hate; pointing finger, temper; third finger, jealousy; fourth finger, lust; etc. Then I asked this six-foot two-hundred-ten-pound lad who was bigger, his forefinger or himself? He agreed he was. Then he promised to rigidly control that finger by biting it, hitting it or sitting on it when in danger of losing his temper. He would greet me, shaking hands with his left hand holding up his right forefinger and say, "Down boy." He had learned a good lesson.

Charles Kingsley: "Thank God every morning when you get up that you have something to do which must be done, whether you like it or not. Being forced to work, and forced to do your best will breed in you temperance, self-control, diligence, strength of will, contentment and a hundred other virtues which the idle never know."[5]

Dale Carnegie: "If you believe in what you are doing then let nothing hold you up in your work. Much of the best work in the world has been done against impossibilities. The thing is to get the work done."

[5]*Dale Carnegie's Scrapbook.*

Dale Carnegie: "Get busy. Keep busy. It is the cheapest kind of medicine there is on the earth and one of the best."

Alexander Graham Bell: "Know what work you want to do and go after it. The young man who gets ahead must decide for himself what he wishes to do. From his own tastes, his own enthusiasm, he must get the motive and the inspiration which are to start him on his way to a successful life."

Thomas A. Edison said, "I never did a day's work in my life. It was all fun."

Dale Carnegie was right. "Do the hard jobs first. The easy jobs will take care of themselves."

3. *Take time to think.* Remember the source of it all is the creative mind. Gather all the facts you can, lodge them in your mind and take time to meditate. Your stomach takes time to digest your food. Your muscles take lots of time to develop in perfect shape and power, so you must plan to think. I use this plan in my correspondence. If I get no impression of an answer to a letter I place it at the bottom of the stack and take time to think it over. When pressed for a decision by a staff member I find it better to sleep on it unless it's an emergency. Let a hot idea get cold, and if it can generate heat when brought out again, then it's got something.

I no longer read my mail early in the morning. I study, read, research, write from 8:00 till 11:00 — go to the office then and check the mail. Those early morning hours are much better invested thusly.

One of the greatest men I knew, Dr. Julius Hickerson, would never read the paper until noon. His morning began at 6:00 in creative investment. Personal matters were relegated to other hours. No wonder he excelled.

Your Key to Concentration is to organize your productivity thus assuring you will concentrate. You can be successful.

Produces Excitement

The man who will apply himself through concentration of all the forces at his personal command in the short span of this life is almost insane as far as the idle spectators are concerned. But to himself, his associates and family he is an exciting, challenging and wonderfully vibrant person. To him life is worth living. Are you living such a life? You can — if you concentrate.

The corridors of history are filled with the thrilling stories of mediocre men who, awaking from slumber, became outstanding successes by excitement in concentration.

When relaxed a muscle is of little strength. When taut, controlled by tension, that same muscle is enlarged, empowered and achieves the purpose of the master.

This is what happens when concentration excites latent abilities. Uncontrolled excitement exhausts needed energies. Take a rubber band. Loose it is useless. Stretched by the wisdom of control it achieves. Extended beyond practicality it breaks or jets into a hidden corner.

Emerson said, "When I go into my garden with a spade and dig a bed I feel such an exhilaration of health that I discover that I have been defrauding myself all this time in letting others do for me what I should have done with my own hands."

Dale Carnegie: "Are you bored with life? Then throw yourself into some work you believe in with all your heart. Live for it, die for it and you'll find happiness that you had thought could never be yours."

Emerson: "Success in your work, the finding of a better method, the better understanding that insures the better performing is hat and coat, is food and wine, is fire and hose, and health and holiday. At least I find that success in my work has the effect on my spirit of all these."

Successful people are happy people. People with a purpose live longer and certainly live fuller than they who do not know where they are going.

William James: "The man whose acquisitions stick is the man who is always achieving and advancing, whilst his neighbors, spending most of their time in relearning what they once knew but have forgotten, simply hold their own."

Sir Theodore Martin: "Work is the true secret of life. The busiest man is the happiest man. Excellence in any art or profession is attained only by hard and persistent work. Never believe that you are perfect. When a man imagines, even after years of striving, that he has attained perfection, his decline begins."

Dale Carnegie: "That is what every successful man loves: the game. The chance of self-expression. The chance to prove his worth, to excel, to win. That is what makes foot races and hog calling and pie eating contests. The desire to excel. The desire for a feeling of importance."

David Grayson: "Happiness, I have discovered, is nearly always a rebound from hard work. It is one of the follies of men to imagine that they can enjoy mere thought or emotion or sentiment. As well try to eat beauty. For happiness must be tricked. He loves to see men at work. He loves sweat, weariness, self-sacrifice.

"Sometimes I will suddenly have a sense as of the world opening around me, a sense of its beauty and its meaning, giving me a peculiar deep happiness, that's near complete content."[6]

Produces Energy

A mentally excited individual produces so much energy that some can feel their presence beyond the five senses. Dumont says, "The mental atmosphere of the hopeful, expectant individual is composed of vibrations of a hopeful,

---
[6]*Dale Carnegie's Scrapbook.*

cheerful character which tend to impress and affect other persons coming within the field of activity of his personal atmosphere."

Some individuals literally radiate power, vigor and emotional impact and exert a positive healing and invigorating effect on all those people they contact.

Robert R. Updegraff in *All the Time You Need* says there are four forms of energy.

"1. Physical energy. Expended in muscular work, walking, playing, etc.

2. Mental energy. Exerted in brain work, reading, writing, talking, planning, grappling with problems, etc.

3. Nervous energy. Excitement, enthusiasm and emotional expression.

4. Energy of the spirit. Electricity sparks our spirits and gives us a sense of buoyancy. Gives us confidence and assurance. Its source is in religious conviction."[7]

Here is the Key to Success. Concentration brings achievement. There is greater power, strength and ability through concentration.

C. W. Wendle said, "Success in life is a matter not so much of talent or opportunity as of concentration and perseverance."

Edison accounts for his achievement from this source.

Remember Dr. Salk took seven years in a Pittsburgh laboratory to discover the solution to polio.

"All men who have accomplished great things have been men of one unwavering aim; men who have sacrificed all conflicting desires and ambitions to that one aim," so says Orison Swelt Marden.

If you are to do some outstanding purpose in this short life you must apply yourself to the work with such a con-

---

[7]Updegraff, Robert R., *All the Time You Need* (Englewood Cliffs, N. J.: Prentice-Hall, Inc., 1958).

centration of forces as "to idle spectators who live only to amuse themselves, looks like insanity."

Edison said, "I never allow myself to become discouraged under any circumstances. The three great essentials to achieve anything worthwhile are, first, hard work; second, sticktoitiveness; third, common sense."

Benjamin Franklin wrote, ". . . God gives all things to industry. Then plough deep while sluggards sleep and you shall have corn to sell and to keep."

Theodore Roosevelt was strikingly characterized by John Burroughs as being "doubtless the most vital man on the continent if not on the planet today."

Basil Matthews in *Wilfred Grenfell, The Master Marine*, tells us, "There is a sound of splashing on the deck. The doctor, stripped to the skin, has let a bucket down over the side with a rope into the arctic water and pulling it up has poured the glittering cascade over himself in the sparkling morning air. He is a great believer in the healing and strengthening of the whole man that comes through letting the water, the sun and the air play on the naked body.

"Admiral George Dewey once took pride in holding his head under water longer than other boys could. 'Perhaps some boy may have since excelled me in the length of time that he could hold his head under water but my record was unbeaten in my day.' It gave the authority of leadership in all water functions."

Charlemagne was such. "He was so hardy they tell us that he would hunt the wild bull single handed, so strong that he felled a horse and rider with one blow. Add to these external traits a tireless energy, an iron will, a keen love of order and of justice, deep-seated religious instincts and under all an exuberant animal nature: such was the man as he appeared to his contemporaries."

Emory S. Bogardus in his book *Leaders and Leadership* said, "Theodore Roosevelt is another example of endurance par excellence. Again the basic relation of endurance to leadership is clear. His sister cites an almost unbelievable picture of the pace which President Theodore Roosevelt maintained when she accompanied him to the St. Louis Fair in 1904:

" 'I ran steadily for forty-eight hours without one moment's intermission. My brother never seemed to walk at all, and my whole memory of the St. Louis Fair is a perpetual jog-trot . . . I literally remember no night at all. At the end of the time allotted to the Fair we returned to our private car, and I can still see the way in which my sister-in-law fell into her stateroom. I was about to follow her example (it was midnight) when my brother turned to me in the gayest possible manner and said, "Not going to bed, are you?" "Well," I replied, "I had thought of it." (He had told his stenographer to rest that day, so that she was ready to take dictation. He began by reviewing the second and third volumes of Rhodes' History of the United States, which he had read on the trip from Washington to St. Louis.) He never once referred to the books themselves, but ran through the whole gamut of their story, suggesting here, interpreting there, courteously referring to some slight inaccuracy, taking up occasionally almost a page of the materials (referring to the individual page without even glancing at the book), and finally, at 5 A.M. with a satisfied aspect, he turned to me and said: "That is all about Rhodes' History." (Then, he prepared a paper on the Irish Question for Peter Dunne.)'

"Roosevelt rode as much as twenty-four hours without changing horses, or forty hours, changing horses five times. In his case the remarkable endurance was built up through careful training from rather poor health in early manhood. It is endurance which supports a person through the long hours of strain and often maintains him in a leadership position."

In his book, Emory S. Bogardus also spoke of Henry

Ward Beecher: "In Elizabeth City, New Jersey, he was to address a crowd of ruffians who had declared that they would kill him if he attempted to speak there. Surrounded by a loyal band he was ushered into the hall, and to the platform. As he began to speak he said: 'Gentlemen, I have been informed that if I attempt to speak here tonight, I am to be killed. Well, I am going to speak, and therefore I must die. But before you kill me, there is one request that I am going to make. All you who are to stain your hands with my blood, just come up here and shake hands with me before you commit the crime, for when I die I shall go to heaven, and therefore I shall not see any of you again.'"

Bogardus also mentions Samuel Gompers: "When Samuel Gompers was presiding over a heated meeting of the American Federation of Labor held in Albany, New York, he was rushed upon and attacked by a man with a pointed revolver: John Brophy rushed from the rear of the room, scaled the bar, and jumped upon the platform where I was standing. He pointed a revolver at my breast. It was certainly a startling scene. I did not touch the revolver, or make any attempt to touch his hand, but with my left hand I caught the lapel of his coat and extended my right palm forward, and in as emphatic a tone as I could command, said, 'Give me that pistol!' He did not give it to me, and still louder and with all the emphasis I could command, I repeated my demand. At the third repetition, he dropped the pistol into my hand, and then bedlam broke loose . . . . I then protected him from them . . . ."

You can be successful through concentration.

Your Success Checkup

1. What did Hubbard say genius is?
2. List the five-point formula for William Hoppe, Jr.'s excellence in billiards.
3. Robert Updegraff listed four forms of energy. What are they?

3.
SUBCONSCIOUS MIND

The Real You

Your key for today is the subconscious mind. "There is dormant in each human being a faculty, whether it is developed or not, which will enable that particular individual to succeed if the desire for success is present in his conscious mind."[1]

What the mind can conceive and believe the mind can achieve. Now your mind is plural. There are two sections — the conscious mind and the subconscious mind. The conscious mind is the architect, the subconscious mind is the contractor and you are the building. The conscious mind is the seat of reason, of logic and of judgment. The subconscious mind is the seat of power, of intuition, of emotion, of inspiration, of suggestion, of imagination, of memory and of dynamic energy. The practical, powerful use of the subconscious mind was the secret of Henry Ford, of Thomas A.

[1]Bristol, Claude, *The Magic of Believing* (Englewood Cliffs, N. J., Prentice-Hall, Inc., 1948).

Edison, of Marconi, the genius of electricity, Westinghouse, of Andrew Carnegie, of Albert Einstein, and of Charles Kettering. Each knew how to use his subconscious mind.

A great French philosopher has said, "The subconscious mind will not take the trouble to work for those who do not believe in it." You see, the subconscious mind is an amazing mental library, either cluttered like Fibber McGee's closet or beautifully cataloged according to the system or lack of system you used in storing away every thought, every idea or every word you have read, studied or heard. Nothing becomes dynamic until it first becomes specific. Our dreams must be crystalized. We do this through pictures. Anything that impresses you draws a picture in your mind. Ben Sweetland, in his book, *Grow Rich While You Sleep,* calls this mental television.

Now the conscious mind is the television camera. The subconscious mind receives and pictures your goal, while enthusiasm is the transmitting power. The man who can picture himself as president of his company will inevitably be president as he practices the law of success, the persistent achievement of a worthy challenging goal.

Do you wish yourself taking your family to Europe? Then frame the group before Big Ben in London, St. Peter's in Rome, the Eiffel Tower in Paris. Regularly state the benefits with excitement. You'd better order your passport, friend, you're on your way.

A Magnetic Power

Your subconscious mind works like a magnet drawing all of the ingredients together in amazing effectiveness to achieve your persistent picture. In 1955 I bought three lots in Orlando, Florida, on which to build a retirement home. I could picture my family there. In 1962 I moved my family to South Florida, having achieved this pictured goal at age forty. I was twenty-five years ahead of schedule.

Clint Davidson in his book, *How I Discovered the Secret of Success in the Bible,* said, "First you must get a person's favorable attention. Then you must change that attention into real interest in the thing you want to do. Third, you must increase interest until it becomes desire. Fourth, you must change that desire into action."[2] My friends, you can do anything in the world you want to do if you want to bad enough. Use your subconscious mind. You can be successful.

The Three Functions of the Subconscious Mind

You can be successful. Your key for today is the use of the subconscious mind. Now there are three functions of your subconscious mind. The subconscious mind takes orders. The subconscious mind is amazingly creative. And the subconscious mind never rests.

One of life's important laws is action and reaction. The subconscious is constantly reacting to the orders of the conscious mind.

The subconscious has no power of choice. It may modify or even adjust an order from the conscious mind, but it never rebels or rejects that order.

The conscious mind plants the seed. The subconscious mind grows the plant, if energized by positive emotions, or your idea may die if destroyed by negative thoughts. You see, you call the signals. Are your seeds producing?

John K. Williams, in his book, *The Knack of Using Your Sub-Conscious Mind,* uses the illustration of the electric storage battery to describe the subconscious mind. The cells and necessary chemicals receive the current from the generator. The battery accepts the charge of electricity from the generator because that's its nature. The electric energy is stored and returned when needed.

[2]Davidson, Clinton, *How I Discovered the Secret of Success in the Bible* (Westwood, N. J.: Fleming H. Revell Co., 1961).

Dale Carnegie says, "Is giving yourself a pep talk every day silly, superficial and childish? No — on the contrary. It is the very essence of sound psychology."

"Our life is what our thoughts make it." These words are just as true today as they were eighteen centuries ago when stated by Marcus Aurelius.

Mr. Quarterback

Several years ago a young man graduated from the University of Louisville with a brilliant football passing record — but he wasn't known nationally because the University of Louisville isn't known as one of the outstanding football giants of America, though it has consistently good teams. The young man wanted to play pro football but he was dropped from the Pittsburgh Steelers' squad at the summer camp and sent home. He played semipro ball in Pittsburgh, and he would hire boys to go out for his passes. Every waking moment he was constantly trying to improve his passing. He tied an automobile tire from the limb of a tree and had a boy pull it with a rope to stimulate movement and he learned to thread the needle of that football through that tire at twenty yards, thirty yards, forty yards, fifty yards, even sixty yards. Then for the price of one $2.36 telephone call, the Baltimore coach called him and said, "Would you like to come and try out for the team?" And he did. He sat on the bench till George Shaw was injured. Then he was ready. He went in. Johnny Unitas became "Mr. Quarterback." He threw touchdown passes in forty-six consecutive games. You see, my friends, he paid the price. He depended upon his subconscious mind to achieve.

Take a piece of paper. Fold it once. Then again and again. The impression made at the point of the fold soon weakens the fiber of the paper. It will then tear at this point. So is the power of continuous orders to the subconscious mind. With repeated orders come deep and lasting impressions. You can be successful.

Creative Power of the Subconscious Mind

The key is the fantastic creative power of your subconscious mind. Tyron Edwards has said, "There is nothing so elastic as the human mind. Like imprisoned steam the more it is pressed the more it rises to resist the pressure. The more we are obligated and obliged to do the more we are able to accomplish."

Sir James Reynolds once said, "The mind is but barren soil: a soil which is so soon exhausted and will produce no crop, or only one, unless it is continually fertilized and enriched with foreign matter." Now the foreign matter is the conscious mind — the orders of the conscious mind upon the creative power of the subconscious mind. The subconscious mind receives, retains, evaluates and acts on every command of the conscious mind. When the order comes through immediately, research librarians are put to work at the command. They are busy people and have other work to do. If this command is restated over and over then the librarian will realize its importance and give it priority.

The conscious mind is the architect. The subconscious mind is both the contractor and the building material. When the blueprint or picture is clear, concise and regularly commanded by persistent instructions from both the owner and the architect, amazing creativity results. The climate must be cultivated by positive emotions. It's tragic to see construction cease because of hostilities on the job.

Today modern ovens have insulated walls that store heat. Then the heat returns to thoroughly cook the cake through from every side. So does your subconscious mind store all that you have accumulated and encountered and then returns this truth to solve your particular problem.

The only principle that all philosophers of all ages agree

on is this: "We become what we think about." "As he [a man] thinketh in his heart, so is he" (Proverbs 23:7).

Did you hear about the woman who had such a lazy husband that when he died she cremated him, put his ashes in an hour glass, turned it up and said: "Now work, you rascal, work"?

Edward Spencer said, "It is the mind that maketh good or ill, that maketh wretched or happy, that maketh rich or poor."

Incubation

Dr. Charles Kimball, president of the multimillion dollar Midwest Research Institute, says, "Gather all the facts available on any particular problem. Study all the facts from every angle. Then lay the problem aside and begin work on something else. Secondly, return to this problem several days later and you will find that all of the pieces have fitted together in a wonderful solution."[3] You can be successful.

Today we have discovered the basis of coherent light. It seems that all power in all light has been focalized in one single light — that light bulb. That's what happens when we concentrate our subconscious mind on one purpose. We must constantly command our subconscious mind to produce the solution to that problem that's facing us. Positively expect a solution by regularly reinstructing your creative mind. Then like a flash the solution will come. Some people call these flashes hunches. With a trusted, cultivated mind they aren't. They are brilliant flashes of genius. Learn to listen to the flashes and learn to trust them.

Your Creative Mind Never Rests

There are three things about the subconscious mind: It is fantastically creative. It never rests. And it takes orders.

[3]*Our Changing World*, No. 799.

Here we are looking at the power of the subconscious mind that never rests.

On October 4, 1963, the *Time* Magazine cover story was on Charles Bates "Tex" Thornton, who in just ten years as president of his company had developed that small microwave tube company to the one hundredth biggest corporation in America. In that decade sales increased 18,570% and earnings 10,175%. Some twenty of his executives have become millionaires and Thornton himself is worth forty million dollars. How was it done?

Tex Thornton regularly mounts his palomino pony and rides the rugged mountains around Los Angeles. During these hours he is doing his most important work — thinking. This amazing industrialist has learned an important truth on the subconscious mind — it never rests.

In the Bible Proverbs 22:29 says, "Seest thou a man diligent in his business? he shall stand before kings; he shall not stand before mean [obscure] men."

Newton, when asked how he got his discoveries said, "By ceaselessly thinking about them." The subconscious mind never sleeps. It is the section of unceasing activity. The research librarians never leave. The lights are never extinguished.

The conscious mind plants the seed. The subconscious mind is the soil, the water and the fertilizer. Germination is the result.

Relaxation Releases Riches

Several years ago 1400 research chemists were surveyed to determine how ideas came to them. Nearly all related that great discoveries came in moments of relaxation, following intensive application. Ideas arrive on the golf course, while fishing, gardening or some other means of relaxation. Some came at night, in church or on the train. For years I have kept a pocket notebook in my possession at all times and especially by my bedside at night. Many times during the night I am awakened with a marvelous solution.

Thomas A. Edison would catnap on the couch in his office. Amazingly, the flashes of truth would strike fire from the furnace of his rested mind.

One successful executive has said, "I find that I no longer approach important problems as being important, but merely as problems requiring long, slow cooking, like the tougher cuts of meat."

The subconscious mind does not go off on another journey. It is continuing to heat through suggestions, recommendations, new ideas and new evidence. However, the most effective cooking is the slow, steady cooking from the all-direction impact of fireless cooking. Any cake is always better baked in an oven than fried in the skillet. You can be successful. Use your subconscious mind.

Suggestion

We motivate the subconscious mind by constant suggestion. The energizing of your subconscious mind is suggestion.

The constant dropping of water on concrete will inevitably crack the concrete. So drop a thought repeatedly over and over and over again and it will bring fruition.

There are five ways to get across an idea: First the hint, then suggestion, third request, fourth command and finally imperative command. The greater the command and the more numerous the impact the quicker and the greater the result.

John K. Williams says, "Any idea, plan or purpose may be planted in the subconscious mind by repetition of thought and empowered by faith and expectancy."

Adolph Hitler practiced this principle to the detriment of all mankind. He knew that if you state a lie long enough, loud enough and enthusiastically enough, most people will believe it.

Suggestion is the principle of advertising. You would believe that Pike's Peak is the highest mountain in the Rockies from all the publicity it gets. But there are fourteen mountains in Colorado alone higher than Pike's Peak.

Overcomes Pain

When used on yourself suggestion is called auto-conditioning or autohypnosis. I received professional training at one time in hypnosis in order to use posthypnotic suggestion in my own life. Following an automobile accident in 1961 I told myself there was no pain. By the time I had been driven four miles to the nearest doctor I literally was free of pain even though my scalp was lying open. I had told myself through the power of suggestion a certain thing and it became true in my mind.

Dr. Joseph Murphy in his book on the subconscious mind relates the following incident: "A relative of mine went to a crystal gazer in India who told him that he had a bad heart and predicted that he would die at the next moon. He began to tell all members of his family about his prediction and he arranged his will. This powerful suggestion entered into his subconscious mind because he accepted it completely. He died as predicted not knowing that he was the cause of his own death."[4]

Drive into the station with your automobile and buy eighteen gallons of gas. You have two choices. Use it to drive 300 miles or you can put your transmission in neutral, race your motor and burn up every bit of the gasoline and never leave the pump. It's up to you.

Use the power of suggestion to give your subconscious mind orders all the time. You can be successful. It's up to you.

---

[4]Murphy, Joseph, *The Power of Your Subconscious Mind* (Englewood Cliffs, N. J.: Prentice-Hall, Inc., 1963).

Your Success Checkup

1. What is the four-point formula that Clint Davidson states in his book, *How I Discovered the Secret of Success in the Bible*.
2. Please state what Dale Carnegie said about giving yourself a daily pep talk.
3. What are the five ways to get across an idea?

4.
THE ORGANIZED MAN

Fred Smith, one of America's outstanding management consultants once said, "The difference in a good business and a bad business is structure. There must be organized structure. The difference in a good business and a great business is emotional motivation." You cannot build a great business until you first have strong motivation.

Time Is Money

Napoleon said, "In every battle there is a fifteen-minute period in which the outcome is decided. The General who discovers that period of time and acts decisively and intelligently always emerges the victor." Abraham Lincoln was wrong when he said, "All men are created equal." I think he meant to say, "All men are created with equal opportunity and with equal access under the law." We are created with different capacities, with different mentalities, different backgrounds, and we are raised in different environments. There is only one factor that we all have equally — and that is time. How we use this time is the key to success or failure. It's all up to you.

A $5,000 a year man is paid about $2.50 per hour for a forty-hour week. The $10,000 a year man is paid about $5.00 an hour for a forty-hour week. The $20,000 a year man is paid $10.00 an hour for a forty-hour week. The $25.00 an hour man is paid $50,000 a year. Of course, no man ever succeeded in working just a forty-hour week. Directly proportionate to the intensity of our efforts and to the amout of hours we spend on our task do we succeed. The point is definite. Time is money.

The man who goes to work for a company actually leases out for those working hours, his mentality, his personality, his ability, his training, his experience, truly all that he is. Since man was created in the image of and with capacity to know God and be a child of God, the leasing of ourselves makes both time and money of far more significance than we usually acknowledge.

Few people in our world have realized this truth and practiced it more diligently than Frank Bettger, the author of, *How I Raised Myself From Failure to Success in Selling,* and, *How I Multiplied My Income and Happiness in Selling,* and *Benjamin Franklin's Secret of Success.* Frank is so methodical that he even counts the number of times he chews each bite of food, and if you are having dinner with him he will count the number of times you chew your food. I know. He told me one time.

A $25,000 Idea

In his book, *How I Multiplied My Income and Happiness in Selling,* Frank tells this tremendous story: "One day an efficiency expert named Ivy Lee was interviewing Charles Schwab, President of Bethlehem Steel Company. Lee outlined his organization's service to Schwab, and ended by saying: 'With our service, you will know how to manage better.' 'I'm not managing as well now as I know how to. What we need is not more knowing, but more doing; not knowledge, but action. If you can give us something to pep us up to do the things we already know we ought to do, I'll gladly listen to you and pay you anything you ask,' said Schwab. 'Fine,' answered Lee. 'I can give you something in twenty minutes that will step up your action and doing at least 50%.' 'Okay,' said Schwab. 'Let's have it. I've got just about that much time before I leave to catch a train.' He handed Mr. Schwab a blank note sheet from his pocket and said, 'Write on this paper the six most important tasks you have to do tomorrow.' That took three minutes. 'Now,' said Lee, 'number them in the order of their importance.' Schwab took five minutes for that. 'Now,' said Lee, 'put this paper in your pocket and the first thing tomorrow morning look at item one and start working on it until it is finished. Then tackle item two in the same way; then item three, and so on. Do this until quitting time. Don't be concerned if you have only finished one or two. You will be working on the most important ones. The others can wait. If you can't finish them all by this method, you couldn't have with any other method either; and without some system, you'd probably not even have decided which was the most important. Do this every working day. After you've convinced yourself of the worth of this system, have your men try it. Try it as long as you wish, and then send me a check for what you think it is worth.'

"The whole interview lasted about thirty minutes. In a few weeks Schwab sent Lee a check for $25,000 with a letter saying: 'The lesson was the most profitable from a money standpoint that I have ever learned.' In five years this plan was largely responsible for turning the unknown Bethlehem Steel Company into the biggest independent steel producer in the world. And it helped make Charles Schwab a hundred million dollars and the best known steel man in the world."[1]

[1]Bettger, Frank, *How I Multiplied My Income and Happiness in Selling* (Englewood Cliffs, N. J.: Prentice-Hall, Inc., 1954).

In this excellent book that I would urge you to buy and keep in your permanent library Frank Bettger goes on to tell about how he set aside the hours on Saturday from 8:00 A.M. to 1:00 P.M. or all day, if necessary, to organize himself for the next week. Between 10:00 and 12:00 each day he phoned for appointments; then he planned to arrange for ten closing appointments a week. Frank goes on to say that he improved every week over the week previous. Later he was able to move his self-organization day to Friday morning, taking the rest of the week off and not worrying about any business until the following Monday morning.

At twenty-nine Frank Bettger, in his first insurance business, was down and out and ready to quit. Yet twelve years later, at forty-one years of age, he was in a position to retire. He gives all of the credit to what he calls his *Self-organizer,* a thirteen week program of organizing himself so he became one of America's outstanding, inspirational leaders and the most dynamic personality that I have ever known.

Destroy Time Thieves

Vernon Howard in his book, *Success Through the Magic of Personal Power,* tells us that there are some time-thieves that will destroy us if we don't kick them out of our lives. No one will allow a thief to remain in his till, his cash register, or in his safe, so you must not allow these thieves to be in your life. Here they are as Howard states them: (1) Lack of self-confidence toward your goal. (2) Playing around the edges instead of plunging ahead. (3) Permitting a contrary desire to weaken your principal purpose. (4) Indecision. (5) Thinking of what you have missed rather than what you could have. (6) Failure to think in terms of personal participation in prosperity.

Disraeli has said, "He who gains time gains everything." And Goethe said, "One always has enough time, if one will apply it well."

Senator Strom Thurmond of South Carolina wears only brown suits and brown ties because he has learned that he saves many hours each year by not having to make a decision over which color suit to wear and which color tie, etc. each morning.

Cerami in his book, *Successful Leadership in Business,* gives us an excellent formula on how to organize our business day: "(1) Organize your day by definite plan. (2) Take advantage of your own natural ebb and flow of energy by setting the hardest tasks for your best hour. (3) Put similar or complementary activities together in a natural sequence."[2]

Six Years More

Do you realize what would happen to your life if you could salvage but one hour a day and invest that hour in personal improvement, or in greater application to accomplish the tasks that are before you? One hour saved each day of a five-day week is worth six years of perceptive effort in a lifetime. At $10,000 a year salary that is $60,000 more to place in your estate, to leave to your family, or to give to a wonderful church or benevolent cause.

How do you so successfully waste time? Could it be through some of these activities: (1) Failing to be decisive about getting up, dressing, eating breakfast, and getting to the office; (2) reluctantly starting on the day's work; (3) letting the wind of circumstance frustrate your creativity by failing to have a plan; (4) wasting precious time in idle conversation, staying twenty minutes when five would have accomplished the task; (5) doing menial tasks that a secretary, custodian, or clerk could accomplish just as well; (6) spending thirty minutes instead of fifteen minutes at the coffee break (fifteen extra minutes at the coffee break each

[2]Cerami, Charles, *Successful Leadership in Business* (Englewood Cliffs, N. J.: Prentice-Hall, Inc., 1955).

week amounts to a week and a half of work time spent foolishly and unnecessarily over a year's time); (7) taking an extra half hour for lunch?

Master yourself and then you can master time. And remember, no man can be master over others, their responsibilities, and their destinies until he has first mastered self and time.

Upper Bracket Income

Earl Nightingale says that the difference between a $50,000 a year executive and a $10,000 a year executive is simply the value of time. A $50,000 a year man has learned how to use several $10,000 a year men, each responsible over dozens, and yea, hundreds of others of lower economic echelon to build an organization that makes the president worth $50,000 a year.

Francis Bacon said, "Time is the greatest innovator." And Baltasar Gracian said, "Nothing really belongs to us but time which even he has who has nothing else." Vauzenargues stated, "You are not born for fame if you don't know the value of time." And Ralph Waldo Emerson declared, "God had infinite time to give us; but how did He give it? In one immense tract of lazy millennium? No, but He cut it up into a neat succession of new mornings, and with each, therefore, a new idea, new inventions, and new applications." And George Gissing points out, "Time is money — says the vulgarest sage known to any age or people. Turn it round about and you get a precious truth — money is time."

Lord Byron said, "It is hoped that, with all modern improvements, a way will be discovered of getting rid of bores; but it is too bad that a poor wretch can be punished for stealing your handkerchief or glove, and that no punishment can be inflicted on those who steal your time, and with it your temper and patience, as well as the bright thought that might have entered your mind, if they had not been frightened away by the bore." Lavater stated, "The great rule of moral conduct is, next to God, to respect time." Benjamin Franklin said, "Dost thou love life? Then do not squander time, for that is the stuff life is made of." Byron declared. "No man can make the clock strike for him the hours that are passed." And Young said, "Tomorrow is the day when idlers work, and fools reform, and mortal men lay hold on heaven." Marcus Antoninus has said, "Every man's life lies within the present; for the past is spent and done with, and the future is uncertain." It was Kerr who said, "Live this day as if it were the last." And Marcus Aurelius said, "Thou wilt find rest from vain fancies if thou doest every act in life as though it were thy last." He also pointed out: "Time is a sort of river of passing events, and strong is its current; no sooner is a thing brought to sight than it is swept by and another takes its place, and this too will be swept away." Thoreau said, "As if you could kill time without injuring eternity." And Queen Elizabeth's last words were, "All my possessions for a moment of time."

At the height of a hard fought battle when Napoleon was leading his forces in Italy, one of Napoleon's generals reported to the emperor and pleaded for more help. Napoleon listened impatiently to a few words and then said, "I will give you anything you ask, except more time."

Yes, time is money — your money, your family's money, money for your retirement years, money you need for investment, money you need for emergency — so begin right now to make a habit of succeeding by acknowledging that every moment is precious, yea, even priceless.

Time Is Available

An ancient Chinese proverb reads, "An inch of gold will not buy an inch of time." Gold will not buy time, but there are ways we can multiply our time by increasing our efficiency through the use of time. Actually, we are buying time many ways.

1. *Printed material gives us more time.* The furniture store that buys a quarter-page ad in a prominent metropolitan city buys time when 50,000 people see that ad. The pastor of the church buys time by sending out a mimeographed or printed letter to the 500 families of his congregation. It would take him many months to visit every one of these families. Furthermore, he buys time by the announcements in the church bulletin that is either used on Sunday or passed out during the week or both. The school principal buys time by mimeographing a notice to the parents about an important matter and handing it out to each child as he leaves the school in the afternoon. The politician buys time by printing posters and billboards and other means of getting his message out before the people. The national product buys time by the use of television and radio in merchandising the product across the nation or around the world. The author buys time by meticulously preparing his manuscript, submitting it to the publisher — then they come together to produce the product that uplifts, challenges and inspires wherever it is read. The executive buys time by dictating letters to his secretary either at his study at home, his office, or oftentimes in the automobile, on the plane, or in other means through portable dictating machines.

2. *The telephone is a marvelous instrument of buying time.* I have found that I can call approximately twenty people in an hour's time. I find that with about 10% of these the lines will be busy, from 25% to 40% will not be at home, depending of course on the time of day that you call. You usually can contact about ten times as many people by telephone as you can by personal calls. I have found that the conference telephone call by lining up several individuals over the same matter over the phone, each in his different

location, is a tremendous asset in buying time. Now with nationwide low rates after particular hours you can accomplish so much at a tremendous saving by using the telephone. Remember, your personality has only partial limitation over the phone over against a personal call. You can project yourself through the telephone in a manner impossible on the printed page.

Shrinking the Globe

3. *Amazing improvements in transportation allow us to buy more time.* Recently I left Miami by jet at 8:00 P.M. and arrived in Bogota, Columbia, South America at 11:00 P.M. The airlines have set up schedules so that a man can leave his office in St. Louis, fly to Atlanta, Chicago, New Orleans, or Denver, transact his business, catch a late afternoon flight and be back in St. Louis well before bedtime. If you have any question about this just ask the manager of the large downtown hotel. They will assure you it is true. Business suffers in the downtown hotel because of the increased travel made available by these jet schedules. You will find that it is quicker, and in the long run, cheaper to rent a car and drive to your destination than to depend upon friends or taxi transportation in most situations. Recently I joined a flying club, some thirty men that own three private planes. On one trip we flew 300 miles in an hour and half, rented a car, made seven business calls, returned the car, climbed aboard the plane, flew back in an hour and half, arrived back home in a shorter schedule than the average working day. It was definitely safer, cheaper, faster, more effective and less tiring than driving or going by train.

4. *You can buy time in shopping by using the telephone.* I have found it far wiser to pick up the phone and call several places to find out if they have the particular product I have in mind than starting out and visiting all of these and consuming greater amounts of time.

5. *We buy time by hiring someone else to do chores that we either do not have adequate time to do or cannot do as effectively as someone else.* For $15.00 a month I can hire a gardening service, a yard service, to cut my grass, fertilize it at certain times, trim the grass around the sidewalk and driveway and around the flower beds, haul away broken limbs and dead branches, as well as advise me when I need new trees, shrubs, or plants — or need old ones removed. Not only have I saved in not having to invest two or three hundred dollars in all the equipment necessary, but I save when this man and his assistant can come in and do the work in a much shorter period of time than I can. Furthermore, my time is worth three or four or five times his time.

6. *We buy time when we read* Reader's Digest, *when we read the daily newspaper, when we read the weekly news magazines and other media that condenses for us the deeper books and materials of the day.*

7. *The housewife buys time when she buys packages of food stuff already prepared*—the instant beverages, the many types of minute baking mixes, the frozen dishes, etc. Dr. Herb True says that one national product of National Food Company has come out with a product called, "Scratch." It is for the sensitive wife whose husband is complaining about her baking things out of boxes rather than developing it completely herself. Now all she needs to do is to tell him I made it from "Scratch"!

Mr. Charles G. Mortimer, President of General Foods Corporation, says that the average German housewife spends six hours a day in her kitchen preparing the meals for her family. But in the United States it is one and a half hours for the same task. No housewife wants to go back to the time-consuming drudgery of building complete meals when from our grocery store shelves we can save time through these marvelous products.

8. *I have bought time of amazing proportions through*

the 3500 volumes in my personal library. Each of these tells me how someone else has done it. I have bought their time, their influence, their mental achievements. Thomas A. Edison said, "I start where the last man left off." You can buy time. Time is available for you. Ralph Waldo Emerson wrote, "Money is of no value; it cannot spend itself. All depends upon the skill of the spender." The same thing is true of time. We have so much. We can spend it wisely or we can dissipate it away. It's up to us. The average person who has lived to be seventy years of age has spent his time in the following manner: three years in education, eight years in amusement, six years in waiting, eleven years in working, twenty-four years in sleeping, five and a half years in washing and dressing, six years in walking, three years in conversation, three years in reading, and only six months in church. Maybe that last one — only six months in church — is the reason for the dangerously increasing crime wave in America.

Robert Ripley, the *Believe It or Not* man, once said, "A plain bar of iron is worth $5.00. The same bar of iron, when made into horseshoes, is worth $10.50. If made into needles, it is worth $355. If made into pen-knife blades, it is worth $3,285, and if turned into balance springs for watches, that identical bar of iron becomes worth $250,000." Can you imagine a better illustration of mastering the use of time? A General Motors executive who makes $250,000 a year has no more time than a day laborer who makes $2,500.

Everyone Has This Capital

Let's picture our time as capital. By learning to spend it wisely we can increase it amazingly. Michael Gore, in his book, *How to Organize Your Time,* says that the proper use of time can increase our working capital by five hundred hours or more than twelve forty-hour weeks each year. That's three extra months of time. Wouldn't it be great if you had it? Gore says: "(1) Define your goal. (2) Work out a definite program. (3) Set up time tables. (4) Concentrate on efficiency." For years I've carried a pocket datebook on my person at all times. It has helped me tremendously to set engagements, to set deadlines, and to schedule my work. I keep a desk calendar and datebook on my office desk and another one on my study desk at home. These are for five years in advance. I set deadlines to meet certain engagements. Let me assure you it helps tremendously.

Here are some of the values of deadlines: (1) You challenge yourself to produce more. Roger Bannister set his goal for the four minute mile, conditioned himself psychologically and physically to do the job, and then trained himself rigidly until he could run the quarter at a certain speed, the half at a certain speed, the three-quarter at a certain speed, therefore making a four minute mile. He had men at each point telling him what his time was, shouting him the time as he went by. These deadlines enabled him to achieve this goal. (2) Discipline your body so that you are able to pay the price. A rigid physical fitness program will drive away many illnesses. It's been many years since I lost a full day's work over illness. The taking of vitámins and proper nutrition, the regular scheduling of constructive, creative physical activities to keep your body under control will enable you to reach your deadline. (3) Reward yourself for each achievement. Visualize your goal at each deadline and you will find it to be an exciting, challenging game. Each segment will vibrantly live. (4) Gather all the facts you can for each deadline. (5) Don't let interruptions take the valuable deposits from your time bank. Be firm and sometimes blunt with those who would unnecessarily consume your time. (6) When mishaps do occur that are uncontrollable, then, if necessary, change or postpone your deadline; but wherever possible, double up to reach your deadline. This gives you a sense of real achievement and joy when you know you have been able to meet it on schedule even though it meant extra effort.

Make Time Deposits

Now if you could draw from your time bank, you must make time deposits. In his record and script on, *How to Master Time Organization,* Paul J. Meyer, President of Success Motivation Institute, Inc., gives us a marvelous means of building time deposits: "(1) By reading, by research, through our education we are storing up time capsules for future use. Ask yourself, Are you investing the time you are now expending for the best possible use? Is it being wasted only on immediate entertainment? Or is it being wisely expended, invested in that wholesome, creative, productive means that will bring forth results down through the years ahead? (2) Have a personal idea file. Maintain a file box and a supply of three by five cards and write down ideas as they come to you. (3) Have a notebook and maintain a day by day record of your accumulated experience in that notebook. (4) Use on the spot dictation with a portable dictating machine. (5) Use your waiting time and all of us have much of this. When you are in the doctor's office, waiting for the delayed plane, waiting for an appointment, waiting for your wife for dinner don't be a time waster; be a time depositor."[3]

Arnold Bennett, in his book *How to Live on Twenty-four Hours a Day,* said, "Philosophers have explained fate. They have not explained time. It is the inexplicable raw material of everything. With this, all is possible; without it, nothing. The supply of time is truly a daily miracle, and a fair genuinely astonishing when one examines it. You wake up in the morning, and lo, your purse is magically filled with twenty-four hours of the unmanufactured tissue of the universe of

[3]Meyer, Paul J., *How to Master Time Organization* (Success Motivation Institute, 1964).

your life. It is yours. It is the most precious of possessions. A highly singular commodity, showered upon you in a manner as singular as the commodity itself."[4]

Four Forms of Energy

The people who waste time are those who do not understand energy. Now there are four forms of energy. When we understand them, control them, use them, make them our slaves, bring them under rigid control of our wills, then we have more time.

The first is physical energy. The second is mental energy. The third is nervous energy. The fourth is energy of the spirit, emotions, the spiritual, the altruistic and the desire for fellowship with God and for service of God and others.

Robert C. Shore, the Chairman of the Psychology Department of Northwestern University, has said, "Successful people are not people without problems. They are people who have learned to solve their problems." The greatest problem many people have is how to use their time effectively.

Horace Mann said, "Habit is a cable; we weave a thread of it every day, and at last we cannot break it." There are five known realities of the universe. These are: (1) Time. (2) Space. (3) Energy. (4) Matter. (5) Intelligence. The man who can fix the habit of using his time effectively and efficiently is the man who will be successful. Habit implies a settled disposition or tendency due to repetition; or custom and custom suggests the fact of repetition rather than the tendency to repeat. We do many things mechanically from force of habit. The next thing you do, determine and commit yourself to establishing a firm habit of using your time productively. You can double your income and double your habit by controlling your time.

[4]Bennett, Arnold, *How to Live on Twenty-four Hours a Day* (New York: Doubleday, 1934).

New Zest in Life

Frank Bettger, in his book, *How I Raised Myself From Failure to Success in Selling*, tells of an interview with Mary Roberts Rinehart, the author of many novels and one of the highest paid writers in America. Here is her answer, "I always thought I could learn to write, if I just had the time, but I had three small sons, and my husband to look after. Also my mother, who for several years was a helpless invalid. Then, during a financial panic, we lost everything. I was driven frantic by debts. I made up my mind I was going to earn some money by writing, so I made up a schedule, planning every hour for the week in advance. Certain periods during the day and in the evening after I got the children off to bed while Dr. Rinehart was out making calls, I set aside for writing."

Frank Bettger asked Mrs. Rinehart if working on such a tight schedule didn't wear her down. "On the contrary," she smiled, "my life took on new zest."[5] And so will yours by organizing yourself. The time is available but you must learn to use it. Andre Gide said, "Our judgment about things vary according to the time left to us to live — that we think is left us to live." And Marcel Prust said, "In general, when we are looking forward to doing something, the shorter the time is the longer it seems to us — because we measure it in shorter units or simply because we think of measuring it."

You can make a habit of succeeding by realizing that all the time you need to accomplish any given task is available to you — but you must master time.

Stretch Your Time Through Planning

The most common factor in all of life is time. We all have the same amount. The vast majority of people dissipate this precious commodity while only a fraction stretch it, enlarge it, expand it, and master themselves and master

[5]*Ibid.*

money and master life, because of their proper use of time.

In his book, *All the Time You Need*, Robert Updegraff says that there are four common enemies of time. One is procrastination. The greatest stumblingblock in the path of most men is not laziness or lack of will nor fear but the attitude of waiting until tomorrow. The second common enemy of time is sometime. The third common enemy of time is the habit of excusing our inactions. And the fourth common enemy of time is regretting. Emerson said, "Finish each day and be done with it. You have done what you could. Some blunders and absurdities no doubt crept in; but forget them as soon as you can. Tomorrow is a new day; begin it well and serenely, and with too high a spirit to be cumbered with your old nonsense." And Cyrus H. K. Curtis encompasses his entire philosophy in four words, "Yesterday ended last night."

Four Enemies of Energy

Updegraff also lists the four common enemies of energy. They are: Frustration. The dictionary calls this, "to fail in attainment, to be baffled, to be foiled, to be defeated." The second common enemy of energy is irritation. The third common enemy of energy is impatience and the fourth common enemy of energy is worry.

Now in this section we are going to show you how you can stretch your time through proper planning. You can cultivate a habit of succeeding.

The first thing to do is to analyze your present time schedule. This means for the next thirty days you need to have a complete analysis of how you are spending your time. Take a legal size sheet of paper, and on the long side start in thirty minute intervals, beginning at 6:00, then the next column will be 6:30, 7:00, 7:30, 8:00, 8:30, etc. throughout the day from the time you get up in the morning until time you normally retire at night. Now on the short side of the paper draw lines and list in the thirty minute squares exactly what you did during that segment of time. For instance, on the short side you may have "telephone." Then you check in every thirty minute segment the number of telephone calls you made or received. Then list encircled the length of each telephone call. Keep a daily record, filing away the sheet as you used it each day. "Oh," you say, "it's time-consuming." That's right. But it's also a time saver.

Now at the end of the month go back and analyze very carefully what your major responsibilities are, and how much time you spent on those major responsibilities. Then analyze how much time you wasted, how much time you spent on activities that should have been delegated to someone else. Now you have an efficient tool to show you how you've been wasting your time.

During college days my next door neighbor, who went on to medical school and is now a prominent physician, made the comment about the difficult days of medical school. A graduate told him that in med school they "threw the work at you." The person who could budget his time and could rigidly stick to that schedule and who would balance his daily schedule with some regular physical activity such as an hour of tennis each afternoon would be able to finish. The graduate said, "The one who can't budget his time and who gets behind in his courses soon flunks out." Several years ago I bought a reading rate machine and doubled my reading rate by using this machine. In one month's time I doubled my reading rate. President John F. Kennedy developed a fabulous reading rate through a speed reading course. This is another example of the effective use of an educational instrument to improve your efficiency.

Plan to Improve

As you analyze your use of time, question yourself carefully as to how much time you spend in your program of personal improvement. How much time do you spend in worthy entertainment? Realize that no man ever succeeded on a forty-hour week — that no man ever became successful unless he paid the price of many long hours in intensive effort. No bank ever succeeded unless the president took it to bed with him at night. It requires the extra effort. Are you willing to pay the price of a program of self-improvement in order to succeed?

How do you spend your average day? Let's look at your time budget: Sleep, eight hours; many get by on less. I'm personally convinced that six and a half hours at night and a thirty-minute nap after lunch or before dinner will do you more good than eight consecutive hours in the middle of the night. Eight hours in one's vocation; four hours for recreation and family enjoyment. That gives you twenty hours. Why not invest those last four in something like this: one hour in the service of God and others through the church, to a benevolent family, in a Boy Scout troop, serving a Boy's Club or coaching a boy's team in an athletic meet and three hours in a program of personal improvement. Have you had the Dale Carnegie course? Then you ought to take it. Begin with the speech course, then the sales course. It will help you tremendously. The Napoleon Hill Foundation has now sold franchises across the nation for a program of personal improvement that is fabulous. Then there is the local adult education program in most cities in America. And through records, through books, and other printed matter you can become a successful person. Let me recommend to you the Great Book series. You can get a liberal arts education by just one hour a week of reading.

A Joke Worth Trying

Napoleon Hill in his book, *How to Sell Your Way Through Life,* said, "Here's a good joke to play on your employer:

get to your work a little earlier and leave a little later than you are supposed to. Handle his tools as if they belonged to you. Go out of your way to say a kind word about him to your fellow workers. When there is extra work that needs to be done, volunteer to do it. Do not show surprise when he gets on to you and offers you the head of the department or a partnership in the business, for this is the best part of the joke."[6]

Frank Bettger quotes Henry L. Doherty, the great industrialist as saying, "I can hire men to do anything but two things, think, and do things in the order of their importance." Remember the $25,000 idea that we mentioned earlier in this chapter? All right, practice that principle with your prospects for the next week. List in order of importance, grading your best prospects "A, B, C, D, and E." Then organize your week to reach these best prospects. Forget that $5.00 account and call on that $500 account. Plan to see some new prospects every week so that you will have some "A" prospects a month from now. But above all, schedule your week well in advance so you will know exactly what to do and let nothing break your schedule.

Master Self

Napoleon Hill said, "Make excuses for the shortcomings of others, if you wish, but hold yourself to a strict accountability if you would attain leadership in any undertaking." No man can rise to fame and fortune without carrying others along with him. Edmund Burke said, "Good order is the foundation of all good things." And Immanuel Kant was a tremendous example of system and organization in life. He said, "I fear every slight change, they will interfere with my health and ruin my study. I must be firm with myself and be methodical in everything I do." Clay Hamlin said, "The

---

[6]Hill, Napoleon, *How to Sell Your Way Through Life* (Cleveland: Ralston Pub. Co., 1958).

beginning of definiteness is the end of confusion." Goethe said, "We always have time enough, if we will but use it aright." And Seneca said, "The greatest loss of time is delay and expectation, which depend upon the future. We let go the present, which we have in our power, and look forward to that which depends upon chance, and so relinquish a certainty for an uncertainty."

It was David Hume who said, "A man's time, when well husbanded, is like a cultivated field, of which a few acres produces more of what is useful to life, than expensive provinces, even of the richest soil, when overrun with weeds and brambles." And Marcus Aurelius said, "The greatest part of what we do or say being unnecessary, if a man takes this away he will have more leisure and less uneasiness. Accordingly on every occasion a man should ask himself: 'Is this one of the unnecessary things?' Now a man should take away not only unnecessary acts, but also unnecessary thoughts, for thus the superfluous acts will not follow after."

All these men are saying is that the man who will challenge time, who will assault time, who will aggressively attack time as being precious and as being a vital tool to succeeding will inevitably succeed. We must ask ourselves the question, "What is the most important thing I can do with this precious segment of time? And will my ultimate goal be achieved in what I'm planning to do with the next period of time?"

Ben Sweetland in his book, *I Will*, tells us that there are two different types of energy, potential and kinetic. Potential energy is energy existing in possibility, but not in actuality. Kinetic energy is energy in motion. Now we all have potential energy, but let's turn our potential energy into kinetic energy by putting ourselves into motion. While you are sitting at your desk trying to decide what to do you are in the area of potential energy, but once you have assaulted the task then you are in kinetic energy.

Elizabeth Akers Allen in, *Rock Me to Sleep,* said, "Backward, turn backward, O time in your flight; make me a child again just for tonight." Wouldn't that be wonderful — but it is impossible, so we must take the time that we now have and go on from here, repenting of the past failures, resolving to change the pattern into fruitful expenditures of this valuable commodity we all have — time. Chesterfield said, "I recommend you to take care of the minutes so the hours will take care of themselves." And someone else has said, "In time take time while time dost last, for time is no time when time is past." Chesterfield once said, "Know the true value of time, snatch, seize, and enjoy every moment of it. No idleness; no laziness; no procrastination: never put off till tomorrow what you can do today." Chilton said, "Once in Persia reigned a king who upon his signet ring engraved a maxim true and wise, which if held before the eyes gave him counsel at a glance fit for every change and chance. Solemn words, and these are they: even this shall pass away."

Benjamin Franklin once said, "One today is worth two tomorrows." Dryden in his *Imitation of Horace,* said, "Happy the man, and happy he alone, he, who can call today his own: he who, secure within, can say, tomorrow, do thy worst, for I have lived today." And Edward Young said, "Time wasted is existent; used is life." Samuel Johnson declared, "Catch, then, O catch the transient hour: improve each moment as it flies; life's a short summer, man a flower; he dies — alas, how soon he dies." And Chesterfield said, "The value of time is in everybody's mouth, but in a few people's practice." Henry Wadsworth Longfellow stated, "Our todays and yesterdays are the blocks with which we build."

What Life Is Made Of

Benjamin Franklin also said, "Dost thou love life? Then

do not squander time, for that is the stuff life is made of."
And James Mason reminds us, "As every thread of gold is
valuable, so is every moment of time." Bacon said, "To
choose time is to save time." And Franklin said again, "If
time be of all things most precious, wasting time must be the
greatest prodigality since lost time is never found again;
and what we call time enough always proves little enough.
Let us then up and be doing, and doing to the purpose; so
by diligence shall we do more with less perplexity."

Baxter once said, "Spend your time in nothing which you
know must be repented of; in nothing on which you might
not pray the blessing of God; in nothing which you could
not review with a great conscience on your dying bed; in
nothing which you might not faithfully and properly be
found doing if death should surprise you in the act." Young
declared, "Youth is not rich in time, it may be poor; part
with it as with money, sparing; pay no moment, but in
purchase of its worth; and what it's worth, at death's bed
they can tell." And Quarles said, "Make use of time if thou
lovest eternity; yesterday cannot be recalled; tomorrow cannot be assured; only today is thine, which if thou procrastinate, thou losest; and which lost is lost forever. One today is
worth two tomorrows." Jay Foster stated, "Keep forever in
view the momentous value of time; aim at its worthiest use
— its sublimest end; spurn, with disdain, those foolish trifles
and frivolous vanities, which so often consume life, as the
locust did Egypt, and devote yourself, with the ardor of a
passion, to attain the most divine improvement of the human
soul. In short, hold yourself in preparation to make the
transition to another life, whenever you shall be claimed by
the Lord of the world."

"There is a time to be born, and a time to die," says
Solomon, and it is a momento of a truly wise man; but there
is an interval between these two of infinite importance.
And Addison has said, "The hours of a wise man are length-

ened by his ideas, as those of a fool by his passion. The time of the one is long, because he does not know what to do with it; so is that of the other, because he distinguishes every moment of it with useful or amusing thoughts; or, in other words, because the one is always wishing it away, and the other always enjoying it." Colton reminds us, "Much may be done in those shreds and patches of time, which every day produces, and which most men throw away, but which nevertheless will make at the end of it no small deduction from the life of man." Milton has said, "Hours have wings and fly up to the Author of time and carry news of our usage. All our prayers cannot entreat one of them either to return or slacken its pace. The mistakes of every minute are a new record against us in heaven. Sure if we thought thus we would dismiss them with better reports, and not suffer them to fly away empty or laden with dangerous intelligence. How happy it is when they carry up not only the passage but the fruits of good, and stay with the Ancient of Day to speak for us before His glorious throne." Benjamin Franklin said, "Improve your opportunities." Said Bonaparte to a school of young men, "Every hour lost now is a chance of future misfortune. Remember that time is money. He that can earn ten shillings a day by his labor and goes abroad or sits idly one half of that day, though he spends but six-pence during his diversion or idleness, ought not to reckon that's the only expense; he has really spent, or rather thrown away, five shillings of time."

Grow Your Time With Care

And Blair said, "Time hurries on with a resistless, un-remitting stream, yet treads more soft than ever did the midnight thief that slides his hand under the miser's pillow, and carries off his prize." Johnson has said, "An Italian philosopher said that time was his estate; and an estate indeed which will produce nothing without cultivation, but will always abundantly repay the labors of industry, and generally satisfy the most extensive desires, if no part of it be suffered to lie awaste by negligence, to be overrun with noxious plants, or laid out for show rather than for use." Mrs. Lydia Sigourney has so well said, "There can be no persevering in industry without a deep sense of the value of time." And Arthur Brisbane said, "Regret for time wasted can become a power for good in the time that remains." And the time that remains is time enough, if we will only stop the waste and the idle, useless regretting.

Colton has pointed out, "Time, the cradle of hope, but the grave of ambition, is the stern corrector of fools, but the salutary counselor of the wise, bringing all they dread to the one, and all they desire to the other; it warns us with a voice that even the sagest discredit too long, and the silliest believe too late. Wisdom walks before it, opportunity with it, and repentance behind it; he that has made it his friend will have little to fear from his enemies, but he that has made time his enemy will have little to hope from his friends." And Goethe said, "It is better to be doing the most insignificant thing than to reckon even a half hour insignificant." Bacon said, "A man that is young in years may be old in hours if he has lost no time." And LeTourneau said, "Be avaricious of time; do not give any value without receiving it in value; only allow the hours to go from you with as much regret as you give your gold; do not allow a single day to pass without increasing the treasure of your knowledge and virtue." Mrs. Sigourney declared, "Lost, yesterday, somewhere between sunrise and sunset, two golden hours, each set with sixty diamond minutes. No reward is offered, for they are gone forever." And Samuel Smiles said, "Lost wealth may be replaced by industry, lost knowledge by study, lost health by temperance or medicine, but lost time is gone forever."

Your Mind Is Showing

Pittman has said, "Well arranged time is the surest mark of a well arranged mind." Bishop Horne advised, "Observe a method in the distribution of your time. Every hour will then know its proper employment, and no time will be lost. Idleness will be shut out at every avenue, and with her, that numerous body of vices, that make up her train." Young said, "Count that day lost, whose slow descending sun views from thine hand no worthy action done." Edward Howard Griggs stated, "No, the river of time sweeps on with regular, remorseless current. There are hours when we would give all we possess if we could but check the flow of its waters. There are other hours when we long to speed them more rapidly; but desire and effort alike are futile. Whether we work or sleep, are earnest or idle, rejoice or mourn in agony, the river of time flows on with the same resistless flood; and it is only while the water of the river of time flows over the mill wheel of today's life that we can utilize it. Once it is passed, it is in the great, unreturning sea of eternity. Other opportunities will come, other waters will flow; but that which has slipped by unused is lost utterly and will return not again."

It was William Penn who said, "There is nothing of which we are apt to be so lavish as of time, and about which we ought to be more solicitous; since without it we can do nothing in this world."

Life Is Worth Living

And Thomas Dreier once said, "If we are ever to enjoy life, now is the time — not tomorrow, nor next year, nor in some future life after we have died. The best preparation for a better life next year is a full, complete, harmonious, joyous life this year. Our beliefs in a rich future life are of little importance unless we coin them into a rich present life. Today shall be our most wonderful day.

"You have to live on this twenty-four hours of daily time. Out of it you have to spend health, pleasure, money, content, respect, and the evolution of your immortal soul. Its right use, its most effective use, is a matter of the highest urgency and of the most thrilling actuality. All depends on that. Your happiness depends on that.

"We never shall have any more time. We have, and we have always had, all the time there is."

Psalm 118:24 says, "This is the day which the Lord hath made; we will rejoice and be glad in it." And Charles Kingsley said, "The men whom I have seen succeed best in life have always been cheerful and hopeful men, who went about their business with a smile on their faces, and took the chances and changes of this mortal life like men, facing rough and smooth alike as it came."

The Organized Life Is More Productive

There is one difference in the $50,000 a year executive and the $10,000 a year executive. The $50,000 a year executive has organized himself to amazingly increase his productivity. The theme of such a man is "A place for everything and everything in its place." These effective methods develop a mind that works like clockwork. Graduates of West Point, Annapolis and the Air Force Academy are always preferred in business because it is impossible for you to be a graduate of one of these academies without learning to organize your time. And Louis Pasteur made note of this in his statement, "Chance only favors the mind which is prepared." J. B. Dumas said of Louis Pasteur, "May Providence long spare you to France, and maintain in you that admirable equipped equilibrium between the mind that observes, the genius that conceives, and the hands that execute with a perfection unknown until now."

Why is the statement, "If you want a job done get a busy man," so generally accepted? The busy man has already learned to organize his time and become amazingly productive. He has a mind that thinks organization, and he can adapt his schedule to achieve the new purpose with only a little bit of increased effort. Napoleon Hill said, "A good encyclopedia contains most of the known facts of the world, but they are as useless as sand dunes until organized and expressed in terms of action."

Remember the saying, "Sow an action and you reap a habit; sow a habit and you reap a character; sow a character and you reap a destiny."

The organized life is a mature, well-adjusted, purposeful, well-balanced, and enthusiastic life. Into this organizational pattern the ingredients of hard work, sound sleep, regular exercise, controlled eating, disciplined conduct, faithful family fellowship, community service, and regular worship — blend them all together in proper proportions and you find outstanding achievement.

A personnel director said to me recently, "I make it a rule not to hire any man regardless of his other credentials who either is in the process of getting a divorce, has recently gotten a divorce, or is untrue to his family." He went on to say such a man did not make it worthwhile for him to secure his services.

Smoking Reduces Production

The president of an outstanding bank told me that he did not hire secretaries or tellers who were undisciplined smokers. He said the bank could not afford to pay them. For the two and three pack a day smoker could not control the habit and spent so much time smoking that it was not profitable to the bank.

A retired physician from one of America's best-known medical clinics told me at a luncheon, "The man or woman without a definite program of physical exercise will shorten his life and is not a good financial risk, either for an insurance company or to the large firm that is looking for top-notch executives."

Recently I counseled with a dear friend whose forty-year-old daughter had committed suicide because her "wheeler-dealer" executive husband had crowded her out of his life. As a direct result of this heartless, cruel conduct the executive had to turn down an executive promotion and assign much of his responsibilities to associates, spend the following two years helping his grieved teen-age children make the necessary adjustments. His lack of organization cost him his opportunity.

A vacationing president of a large multimillion dollar firm said, "I recently passed over one of the most outstanding young men in our organization because he didn't have interest nor time for regular worship. The man who doesn't think he needs God doesn't have the resources to withstand the crises that inevitably come to the men who fill our executive positions."

A Terrible Price to Pay

The estimates run that from 50% to 80% of all hospital beds in America are filled with psychosomatic illnesses as a direct result of disorganization. Psyche means mind; soma means body. When these two pieces of delicate machinery are beautifully and smoothly functioning in harmonious balance, you have wonderful productivity; violate these principles of organization in your personal life and you too may be in the psychosomatic ward. Somerset Maugham wrote, "The common idea that success spoils people by making them vain, egotistic, and self-complacent is erroneous; on the contrary, it makes them, for the most part, humble, tolerant, and kind. Failure makes people bitter and cruel."

Recently I chatted over coffee with the president of the American Alcoholic Rehabilitation Foundation. We discussed how the tremendous mental, scientific, and executive manpower of America is so tragically exhausted, dissipated and destroyed by the disorganization that is rampant in the mind of so many men and women. This alcoholic specialist said that one of every two adults who drinks alcohol is either a chronic alcoholic or an excessive drinker, or on given occasions drinks beyond wise and moderate control. Loss of productivity is inevitably the result. The organized man controls the circumstance, including the drink, rather than letting the drink and the circumstances control him.

Set Time Deadlines

One of the most effective ways of increasing productivity is to set definite time limits on all of your responsibilities. Deadlines, held to as rigidly as possible, do several things: (1) You are stimulated to give your best. (2) You draw from your mind, your body and your emotions, your vast experiences to achieve a specific purpose in an alloted time. (3) You positively control the evils of procrastination, time waste, and unhealthy relaxation of intensity of purpose.

If you have been diligent and faithful in your time analysis study that we previously recommended you will find that you regularly waste many precious hours every day. After studying this analysis carefully, you now want to establish an organized pattern of life that will greatly use these hours that so often are abused and dissipated. What about your evenings, your weekends, your holidays, all the time you spend waiting on someone else, the lunch hours that can so readily be turned into stimulating conversational duels by scheduling the outstanding individuals of your community who, by their very presence and conversation, will tremendously stimulate you to more effective work? Take the next month and plan to associate yourself either in dinner in your home, or going out to dinner, with some of the most interesting, challenging individuals of your community. Don't schedule yourself so rigidly that you can't adjust. Try to keep at least one evening a week free to allow for that unusual circumstance, the sudden phone call of the couple you wanted to learn from and to fellowship with. Use your social engagements as opportunities for personal advancement through the fellowship of the right people.

By all means regularly call on and fellowship with the retired people of your community, your vocation, and your vacationing opportunities. Remember, the retired successful individual delights in sharing all that he has learned with younger friends. He acknowledges his debt to succeeding generations. And, of course, above everything else, schedule your time to do effective and purposeful reading.

Yoritomo Tashi, a great Japanese philosopher, said, "Mistrust of ourselves, the source of timidity, always springs from lack of confidence in our own strength, and must weaken us by hindering us from giving to our thoughts and their realization the inspiration to exalt." If you are not producing because of timidity; if you are not achieving because of lack of aggression; then acknowledge that you have got to change your entire life pattern. Now seize the situation; have done with lesser things; establish a strong reserve of your task, so this may be the force that compensates in future achievements. Rigidly resolve that you are going to pay the price of organizing your life for effective productivity.

Six Steps to Time Mastery

Paul J. Meyer in his record, *How to Master Time Organization,* gives six wonderful steps for mastering time. Here they are: "(1) Make Notes. (2) Remove distractions from your work area. (3) Discourage interruptions. (4) Learn to say no. (5) Learn to listen carefully. (6) Let your postman be your errand boy."[7]

By organizing my thoughts as to how I would react in

---

[7] *Ibid.*

any emergency I was prepared when a tragic automobile accident occurred. I reacted according to the organized pattern that I had previously established. Miraculously, I was spared all but a minor scar. In this case organization not only meant productivity, but organization meant my life. Dale Carnegie has said, "If you have a worry problem, do these three things: (1) Ask yourself, 'What is the worst thing that can possibly happen?' (2) Prepare to accept it if you have to. (3) Then calmly proceed to improve on the worst." James Gordon Gilkey said, "What is the true picture of your life? Imagine that there is an hour glass on your desk. Connecting the bowl at the top with the bowl at the bottom is a tube so thin that only one grain of sand can pass through it at a time.

"That is the true picture of your life, even on a super-busy day. The crowded hours come to you always one moment at a time. That is the only way they can come. The day may bring many tasks, many problems, strains, but invariably they come in single file."[8]

General George C. Marshall said, "When a thing is done, it's done. Don't look back, look forward to your new objective." And Reinhold Niebuhr said, "God grant me the serenity to accept the things I cannot change, the courage to change things I can, and the wisdom to know the difference." Herbert Hoover said, "Never worry about anything that is past. Charge it up to experience and forget the trouble. There are always plenty of troubles ahead so don't turn and look back on any behind you." And Henry Wadsworth Longfellow wrote, "The night shall be filled with music and the cares that infest the day shall fold their tents like the Arabs, and silently steal away." Napoleon said, "When I want to consider a particular problem, I open a certain drawer. When I have settled the matter in my mind,

[8]Carnegie, *Ibid.*

I close that drawer and open another. When I desire to sleep, I close all the drawers."

It was Marshal Ferdinand Foch who said, "I know that I am considered an inveterate optimist and properly so. Why? Because I always turn my eyes toward success, not failure. I involuntarily turn my back on disaster and eliminate the hypothesis of failure. This is my philosophy in action. Every time you have a task before you, examine it carefully, take exact measure of what is expected of you. Then make your plan, and in order to execute it properly, create for yourself a method, never improvise." And William James said, "When once a decision is reached and execution is the order of the day, dismiss absolutely all responsibility and care about the outcome." Benjamin Franklin advised, "Let all your things have their places; let each part of your business have its time." Thomas Carlyle declared, "Our main business is not to see what lies dimly at a distance, but to do what lies clearly at hand." And Dale Carnegie urged, "Get the facts. Let's not even attempt to solve our problems without first collecting all the facts in an impartial manner." Carnegie also said, "Look facts in the face, bitter though they may be: make a decision, and after you have once made the decision, devote all your time to carrying it out. Don't spend any time worrying about whether it is right. Make it right."

When you read the story of the ten most prominent executives in the nation, all whose salaries run $200,000 or more, realize that they have one thing in common — they have mastered their time in order to produce so effectively. You can make a habit of succeeding by organizing your life.

Organize Your Life, Now

This may be the most important thought in all of this book: Your life can be changed by mastering time organization. Benjamin Franklin excelled in so many amazing endeavors because he mastered time organization. Frank Bettger became a $1,000 a night speaker and one of America's outstanding salesmen and writers because he mastered time organization. You can double your production, your income, your happiness, your sense of achievement by mastering time organization. Master the many sub-mediocrities by measuring up to your magnificent obsession.

(1) Determine your purpose. Write out where you want to be and what you want to accomplish for yourself, your business, your family, your church, your community, and your estate at a given period of time, ten, twenty, thirty years from now or at retirement.

(2) Set yearly and probably monthly goals which are check up points on your routes to achievement.

(3) Through your time analysis sheet determine how and where you failed in the past as a result of wasting your time.

(4) Determine how you are going to use all of your associates to help you achieve this program of success. Sit down in a family conference and discuss it with all of the members of your household. Make them your willing allies. Point out how much more you can help them and serve them and meet their needs through the discipline of time organization. Of course, the greatest thing you can do for them is to instill within them the desire for achievement.

(5) Work with your business and civic and church associates. Bring them into your plans only to the necessary point of their cooperation. Remember, many people cannot rise to the heights of enthusiasm, cannot visualize the goals you have set for yourself, therefore to discuss your purposes and goals with the people who do not have the capacity of achievement may be detrimental in that they can become critical or jealous.

(6) Through printed policies and procedures bring these associates into your overall plan. It may be necessary to

eliminate their conscious commitment and participation in your program of achievement. However, they can be unconscious allies as you use their time to help you accomplish more. Remember, never do any task that someone else can accomplish through delegation. Never forget that the idea men are the masters. There are one hundred detail men to every great idea man. You can only achieve your greatest by becoming an idea man. Furthermore, realize that your associates never really began to accomplish their dormant capacities without your challenging them. Most administrators fail to achieve the best with their subordinates because they make them robots rather than develop their innate capacities.

And by all means discipline yourself to secure the education needed to accomplish your purpose. Never forget that the man with eight years of schooling earns an average of less than $3,000 a year. The high school graduate, $6,000 a year; and the college graduate more than $9,000 a year. But stop right there. I know some graduate school graduates with Master's and Doctor's Degrees who are resting on their oars. They have quit achieving. On the other hand a few men who didn't finish high school are fabulously successful because they never stopped learning. In our society there are many night schools located at the metropolitan university or branches of the state university, the amazingly successful correspondence courses in so many areas, the business schools, and by all means the wealth of wonderful books and periodicals that enable any man with desire to accomplish his purpose in life.

Dr. William C. Menninger of Topeka, Kansas, where he and his brother Karl operate the Menninger Clinic, one of the outstanding psychiatric clinics in the world, urges you to get a periodic emotional check-up. Dr. Menninger says in this emotional check-up you should do the following things: "(1) Determine your purpose and goals in life. What do you want to accomplish? (2) Check up on your personal relationships. How are you getting along with people? What is your temperamental quotient? (3) How do you handle emergencies? Can you control your temper? Have you learned to live with tension? Have you learned to expel your tensions by mowing your lawn, by bowling your anxieties down the lane, or by driving them down the golf fairway? (4) Have you selected and do you regularly take part in constructive, creative activities that allow you to expend yourself unselfishily in the service of others? (5) Is your character so well formed that you can be honest, truthful, loyal, and cooperative with others? (6) Do you regularly take your vacation and your time off and use these periods for rebuilding your diminishing emotions, for recharging your excitable battery?"[9]

Set aside some additional hours every day for your program of personal achievement. Do you say, "But I can't get everything done now"? Organize your life and you can get far more done. Take, for example, the person who spends thirty minutes each day going to work. That's an hour a day. This comes to 245 hours a year or the equivalent of thirty eight-hour days. This means you have an extra month every year if you can use this thirty-minute period productively. Those who are on public transportation can spend this time in constructive reading. Sit down and work out a thirty-day program of personal improvement through creative reading. Let me urge you to try to find public transportation. It will save you a great deal of anxiety with the hectic driving that is the pattern of so much of American Urban life. The motto: "Take the bus and leave the driving to us," can be your asset. Or, if it is necessary that you drive your automobile, then secure for yourself a transistorized tape recorder and play tapes about outstanding programs as an investment in your future. Why not secure for yourself, as I

[9]*Our Changing World,* No. 832.

have, a forty-five record player that attaches to your radio? You can play inspirational records as well as put on these records of outstanding learning techniques.

And still another way for wise men to invest their time in learning is sleep learning techniques. Here you attach special mechanisms to your record player with a small amplifier under your pillow and while you are sleeping you will learn as the record speaks to your subconscious mind all that you want to know. Let me assure you it works.

In his book, *The Master Key to Riches,* Napoleon Hill has given us the following chemical development of man: 95 pounds of oxygen, 38 pounds of carbon, 15 pounds of hydrogen, 4 pounds of nitrogen, 4½ pounds of calcium, 6 ounces of clorine, 4 ounces of sulphur, 3½ ounces of potassium, 3 ounces of sodium, ¼ ounce of iron, 2½ ounces of florine, 2 ounces of magnesium, and 1½ ounces of silicon, with small traces of arsenic, iodine and aluminum. This makes up the chemical elements of a 160 pound man. You know how meticulously these must be organized and they must not get out of focus. Actor Bob Cummings says that if you add a little bit of iodine it will keep your hair from turning gray.

So is the organized life necessary to be properly and effectively mastered for achievement. There must be balance; there must be system; there must be cooperative endeavor in order to achieve your purpose in life.

One of the most valuable aids you can ever secure in mastering time organization is to get the record, *How to Master Time Organization,* by Paul J. Meyer, President of Success Motivation Institute, Inc., Waco, Texas. Paul will tell you how to develop a daily time use schedule. Get that record and it can revolutionize your life.

Another valuable book is, *How I Multiplied My Income and Happiness in Selling,* by Frank Bettger, published by Prentice-Hall. Frank has a thirteen week self-organizer program that is amazing. I know of no better tool to help you master time.

The one thing in all this world and the only thing that you totally control is your own mind. You can determine what goes into it and, yes, you can even determine what comes out of it. Your time is like a bank. You can only take out what you put in. You will make time deposits by using time to effectively store away the tremendous truths of personal success. Then these truths will come back to master you and to lead you to succeed. You can make a habit of succeeding.

Your Success Checkup

1. To earn $50,000 a year how much is your time work per hour?
2. What are the six time-thieves Vernon Howard lists in his book, *Success Through the Magic of Personal Power?*
3. What are the six ways many people waste time?
4. What is the four-step formula that Frank Gore assures you will increase your time by three months each year?
5. List the five steps that Paul Meyer states you can use in building time deposits.
6. What are the six reasons why people fail?
7. What are the three effective ways of increasing productivity?
8. What are the six wonderful steps for mastering time that Paul Meyer gives you?
9. Write out the six-point formula Dr. Menninger gives you for your emotional check up.

5.

THE PROBLEM OF FATIGUE AND HOW TO OVERCOME IT

Fatigue is a condition of impairment, resulting from prolonged mental or physical activity or both, usually removable by rest. Sometimes it refers to the organic state of lowered energy following work, other times to the feeling of tiredness or boredom experienced and often to the decline in efficiency of the performance of our work. Fatigue may come upon a person as a result of loss of sleep, fear and emotional strain, cold and high altitudes, or sheer ennui from immobility and endless waiting with nothing to do.

One neurologist said, "In our day, our nerves are bombarded with more stimuli than could be squeezed into an ordinary lifetime a century ago." The complexity of this life is so demanding that many people simply can't cope with the problem.

Marguerite Clark, in her book, *Why So Tired?*, published by Crest, suggests some symptoms of fatigue: "Shoulders drooping, heads bowed, eyes heavy with lack of sleep, headache, insomnia, low energy, poor circulation, irritability, they are all in, beat, fed up, they can't finish a job or what is worse, they can't get started on anything new."[1] One medical dictionary defines fatigue, "A condition of the cells or organs in which through over-activity, the power or capacity to respond to stimulation is diminished or lost." Others said, "Exhaustion of strength, weariness from exertion." "A painful feeling of lassitude caused by work, of a physical or intellectual effort." "An overall disinclination to action." "A disturbance of the balance between wear and tear."

"But what one person can do without becoming exhausted compared to another, is a tremendous variable," said Dr. Robert S. Schwab of Boston, a fatigue expert. "And the energy output of a person under one set of circumstances, compared with the way he handles exactly the same task, but under different conditions, is a second important variable." Dr. Schwab continues, "Chronic fatigue is not the pleasant fatigue that follows a stimulating game of golf or rewarding day at the office or at home, from which the person emerges after relaxation of sleep, feeling like new. Their tiredness is not related to physical exertion. It is all out of proportion to energy spent and will not disappear with rest, sleep, or vacation. This chronic fatigue is a serious threat to health and happiness."

The Executives' Disease

Dr. E. J. Kepler, a Mayo Clinic practitioner, says, "In the main, chronic fatigue is a disease of the intelligentsia. Doctors, lawyers, ministers and their wives, artists, musicians, students, teachers, big and little business men, executives, and white collar workers all grow exceedingly weary. Numbskulls rarely are effected. Those that use their muscles instead of their wits seem to escape abnormal fatigue because

[1]Clark, Marguerite, *Why So Tired?* (Greenwich, Conn.: Crest Books, 1962).

they expect to be tired. Day laborers and charwomen do not seek medical help for the familiar after affects of wielding the picket or the mop."

A husband who has an extended argument with his wife about the financial problems before he goes to work, then receives running harassment all day from his boss at the office is exhausted before he gets home at night from the emotional conflicts brought about by these two extended activities.

Marguerite Clark also quotes Dr. Thomas Keliher, "For practical purposes we can get at least a working concept of the mechanisms of fatigue, both physical and mental, by thinking of the body and brain as a gigantic heat producing furnace governed by a sensitive thermostat in the brain. This thermostat is set with a wide margin of safety, so that energy output is usually cut off long before it is actually necessary to prevent exhaustion. . . . As far as physical fatigue is concerned, scientists know that powerful body chemicals, hormones, and enzymes can set the thermostat higher or lower. Inadequate fuel for the furnace, in the form of weak muscles, low metabolism, and poor blood circulation, causes the alarm center in the brain to turn off the heat, or energy production, sooner than it is desirable, leaving us tired.

"From a psychological standpoint we know that pleasurable excitement and determined will power can move up the thermostat, allowing greater production of energy, and less fatigue. On the other hand anxiety, chronic fear and depression appear to set the thermostat lower, depriving us of our much needed energy, and often leaving us tired before we start to use our bodies and our minds."[2]

Three Kinds of Fatigue

The three categories of tiredness are: (1) Pathological fatigue: This is an early development of what could be an

[2]*Op. cit.*

organic difficulty. (2) Physiological fatigue: This is from chemical reactions in the blood of normal people that leave the muscles dissipated. (3) Psychological fatigue: From intensive emotional conflicts, boredom or frustrations.

The extremely tired individual is like a ship on stormy seas almost swamped by the conflicts of fear of failure at the office, fear of failure in the business, personality conflicts at home or at business, disappointment of children or other relatives, financial crises, fear of replacement in employment because of limited education, or any one of a hundred other emotional conflicts.

If the tiredness is in an early stage then the ship is run aground. A shift in the sand, a change of the tide, or an unloading of part of the cargo will enable the ship to float free and proceed on its path.

Sustained and consistent emotional conflicts are like a ship adrift in the middle of the storm with engine, rudder or other structure defective. Expert engineering skill such as good counseling will help the ship to function effectively again.

Deep and damaging fatigue of many years standing is like the ship frozen in ice. The mental depression means the ship will stay there until the spring thaw or dynamite which is some unusual psychological experience that floats the ship free.

In his book, *How to Live 365 Days a Year*, Dr. John A. Schindler says "that at least 50% of all illnesses today are caused by emotional induced illness." One medical book contains the account of roughly one thousand different diseases that the human body is subject to. Emotionally induced illness is as common as all the other 999 put together.

For example, a few years ago the Ochsner Clinic in New Orleans published a paper which stated that 74% of 500 consecutive patients admitted to the department handling gastro-intestinal diseases were found to be suffering from E.I.I.

Dr. Schindler lists the following complaints and their per cent of occurrence in medical cause: pain in the back of the neck, 75%; a lump in the throat, 90%; ulcer-like pain, 50%; gall bladder-like pain, 50%; gas pain, 99%; dizziness, 80%; headaches, 80%; constipation, 70%; tiredness, 90%.

In 1884 William James said that an emotion was: "A state of mind that manifests itself by sensible changes in the body."

Dr. Schindler says that there are two general kinds of emotions: The over-stimulations. These are called the unpleasant emotions, such as, anger, anxiety, fear, apprehension, discouragement, grief and dissatisfaction. The second large group of emotions are the optimal-stimulations or the pleasant emotions, such as, hope, joy, courage, affection and agreeability.

The problem is that emotionally induced illness is a physical not a mental disease, and our bodies actually suffer when these emotions are unhealthy. Our bodies respond favorably from the pleasant emotions.

Four Signs of Fatigue

There are some very definite facts that warn us when fatigue is taking place: (1) A continued and sustained feeling of tiredness, the inability to snap back after a period of extensive exertion. (2) A steady decline of muscle strength as we continue over a period of time. (3) The inability of the heart rate to recover after particular strenuous activity. If our heartbeat is quickly restored and normal rhythm resumed, then we aren't bothered by fatigue. (4) The effectiveness of our work output. The individual who is suffering from fatigue has a decidedly diminishing pattern of work production.

Some of the feelings that come over the individual suffering from fatigue are exhaustion, pain, suicidal tendencies, claustrophobia, hallucinations, excessive emotionalism, and depression. His attitude toward others will be expressed in hating and being hated, fearing and being feared, doubting and being doubted, failing and feeling inadequate, and finally becoming so.

How to Talk Your Way to Tiredness

Our subconscious minds are the character and the building materials that the architect, the conscious mind, is using to build the building, ourselves. Now, if the conscious mind continues to express negative emotions to the subconscious mind, it is inevitable that fatigue will follow. Here are some suggestive things that bring about fatigue from the conscious mind: "You are working too hard and it is too monotonous." "Your boss is a dictator and drives you like a slave." "The physical conditions around this place are awful and an animal shouldn't have to suffer it." "The people in this plant are devils and no one can get along with them." "There is no way to reach the quota the boss has established for you." "It is a constant strain at the office all the time and there is no rest and peace and happiness when you get home." "You keep this up and you will lose your job and be in a terrible financial situation." "You don't want to work anyway. You hate every minute of it." "You really aren't well and you have an excuse to stay home." "No one loves you. No one gives you any attention or sympathy." "Everybody else is on the government payroll and they owe you a living also." "Some people have an inferiority complex but you are just plain inferior." "Your wife hates you and you hate her and all she wants is what she can get out of you." "Life isn't worth living anyway, is it?"

All of these things are the result of one basic cause — emotional stress. In her book, *How Never to Be Tired,* Marie Beynon Ray says, "Far more of us who say we are tired are not tired at all. We would not be tired at all unless we got under the wretched trick of feeling tired. We are all of us to some extent the victims of a habit neuroses. We live subject to a rest by degrees of fatigue which we have come only from habit to obey."[3]

Dr. William James says, "Men the world over possess amounts of resources which only the very exceptional push to their extremes of use. The same individual pushing his energies to their extreme, may in a vast number of cases keep up the pace and find no bad reaction. The man who energizes below his normal maximum fails by just so much to profit by his chances of life. He could run at a higher pressure and accomplish more. Men habitually use only a small part of the powers which they actually possess and which they might use under appropriate conditions."

Measure Your Energy!

In his book, *Don't Be Afraid,* Dr. Edward Spencer Cowles has developed a chart for measuring nerve cell energy. The person in perfect health registers a hundred. The person from a hundred to eighty is restless, irritable, has morning tiredness, exhilaration later in the day. The person from eighty to sixty has insomnia, inability to concentrate, is despondent, has headaches, heartburn, diarrhea, indigestion, constipation, pains, fears and greater depression. The person from sixty to forty has increased fear, a sense of unworthiness, guilt, a sense of persecution and suicidal thoughts. The person from forty to twenty has blackness spells mingled with high excitement, inability to rest or keep quiet, inability to sleep or eat, and is a very intensive person. The person from twenty to zero has excitement, delirium, exhaustion, coma, and finally death.

With proper rest, the right food, emotional maturity,

[3]Ray, Marie Beynon, *How Never to Be Tired* (Indianapolis: Bobbs-Merrill Co., Inc., 1938).

happy home relationships, creative job productivity, a person will restore his nerve cells full of energy and can face most any stress in life. However, if such creative activity is not a part of the individual's life, fatigue soon becomes dominant and controls and ruins.

If you take a full glass of water and take out one drop each day you will hardly notice it. But if you keep taking out one drop of water a day and putting none in then soon the glass will be one-third empty, one-half and finally two-thirds empty. Then you will find yourself with no water at all. This is a simple illustration of what happens when we fail to restore our energy capacity through normal creative conduct and activity to its full useful source.

I stated earlier that the laborer doesn't suffer from fatigue, that it is the white collar worker, the professional individual, the business executive, the doctor, lawyer, or minister. It is simply because these individuals come under more emotional stress through their normal daily activity than the day laborer.

Dr. Walter C. Alvarez of the Mayo Clinic says, "The highest centers of the brain are the first to fail under the influence of overwork, worry, loss of sleep, and all the other producers of fatigue." It is for that reason that the professional person needs to accept the fact of fatigue and earnestly and sincerely develop a program for the overcoming of this serious problem.

The Causes of Fatigue

While I was seated at my desk writing a chapter in a previous book my boxer dog was hit by an automobile in front of the house. I heard the screech of the tires; I heard the dog bark; I rushed out and found her hobbling across the yard obviously with some broken bones in her hips and maybe her back. Incidentally, the lady who hit her didn't even stop. I put the dog in the car and rushed her to the veterinarian. There he found she had a broken pelvic bone, some other broken hip bones and internal injuries — internal bleeding. After some two or three weeks at the veterinarian's she returned home, though she showed the effects of it for awhile, fully recovered.

During the fighting on the peninsula across the estuary from Naha on the island of Okinawa in April and May of 1945, I remember one of the most brilliant marines in our outfit, a boy from the slums of Manhattan. In training camp he had been a jailbird in the brig about as much as he stayed out, but in combat he proved himself as a brilliant marine. He had gone to battalion headquarters to secure some ammunition. As he was returning to the Company Command Post, a Japanese sniper's bullet hit his hand, went through his wrist, not breaking the bone. It was just a flesh wound which ricocheted off a bazooka shell he was carrying and lodged in his chest over his heart. This man who had been fearless in combat, exposing himself time after time after time in heroic manner, collapsed. Looking at the bullet barely sticking into his chest, he was convinced that it had entered his heart and he fell over dead. The doctors were amazed — a minor flesh wound, not even a broken bone. They pulled out the bullet from his chest with tweezers. It had come nowhere near his heart. He died of fright.

Animals are not bothered by psychological fatigue — only humans. Therefore, our emotions wrongly directed are the main cause of fatigue.

Emotions are wrong only when used in wrong ways. When we let worry control and ruin and destroy us we are admitting that we have become slaves to our emotions rather than making them rigidly our slaves. Remember the words of William James, "The greatest discovery of my generation is that we can alter our lives by altering our attitudes of mind." Worry and fear are the twin demons that soon will destroy. As Dale Carnegie has said, "Face the thing that seems overwhelming and you will be surprised how your fear will melt away."

Diagnose Your Own Tiredness

The three main areas of fatigue are:

(1) *Physical.* This is only temporary. There is no such thing as a fatigue debt. That is, this kind of fatigue cannot pile up. The energy lost during the day is made up for in a good night's sleep. This type of fatigue cannot be carried over to the next day or the next week, that is, if we have proper food and rest and recreation. The word recreation means to re-create our total abilities. Actually fatigue is a God-given protection when it is only physically caused. It warns us to stop our work and get some rest. I remember when our two older children, then two and a half and four, both had their tonsils out the same day. After the able physician had operated in the morning and kept them in his office during the afternoon, we were told we could take them home in the late afternoon. We were a little bit concerned that there might be bleeding during the night and I asked him about that and he said this, "The good Lord has built in marvelous check systems for our health. If the child were to bleed during the night, they would swallow the blood and the stomach would throw the blood up." He said there is no danger, the body will warn us. So it is that fatigue from physical exertion is a warning to stop and get some rest and food and recreation. If you feel physically fatigued ask yourself these four questions: 1. Did I eat the right food, not only today but in recent weeks? Have I had proper nutrition? Of course, eating too much is bad also. 2. Have I had plenty of fresh air and sunlight? 3. Has my physical exercise and recreational activity been wise? 4. How was my sleep the night before and for several nights and have I been working short enough days to allow

my body to snap back? Overwork over an extended period of time will bring about physical fatigue.

Of course, physical fatigue can come through irregular hours of sleep, from impure air in the plant in which you work, from fumes, from dust, etc. Overcrowding, loud noises, and frustrating conditions, even extremes of temperature — cold or hot — may affect your body's thermal-regulating system and limit the amount of the energy your body produces. When you are working under extreme heat you should take more water and you should take salt tablets to make up for what your system is expending. For many years I have been on vitamins. They help me tremendously to make up what my system has been missing. Recently I read an article about the models and how so many of the fashion models actually starve themselves to stay trim. They have physical fatigue. We are told that breakfast is the most important meal of the day, for our work capacity greatly diminishes shortly before noon if we have not had a good meal at breakfast.

(2) *Pathological.* Pathological fatigue is an early symptom of a serious organic disease. In a test made at the Lahey Clinic in Boston among some 300 people with chronic fatigue, Dr. Frank N. Allen found the following pathological involvement in 58 of these 300 people: 12 had hidden infections, 8 heart disease, 8 diabetes, 8 narcolepsy, 5 serious anemia, 4 thyroid disorders, 3 Myasthenia gravis, 3 epilepsy, 1 syphilis, 1 brain tumor, 1 vitamin shortage, 1 lung tumor, 1 unclassified fever and 1 Hodgkins Disease. That's 58 out of 300. Among the other three out of four nothing organic could be found to explain their fatigue.

(3) *Psychological.* A man raised as an only child in a home where his overly protective mother always expected him to be involved in some critical accident or to die from a heart weakened from rheumatic fever or some other situation grew up to marry a neurotic wife who was constantly

overly concerned about his health. Every morning he left to go to work with the final instructions from his wife, "Drive carefully, you may get killed. Fasten your safety belt. Most people are killed within ten miles of home. Don't do anything strenuous it may upset your heart." The automobile agency where he worked brought in a high pressure sales manager who set his goal to double production at all costs. His favorite theme was, "Remember, fellows, one day we won't even get up. Some night we are going to die. Remember every day you are one day closer to the grave. We have got to sell now. Sell! Sell! Sell!" After he was absent three days in a row, this man's wife called the Sales Manager one day and said, "What have you been telling him? For three days he has been in bed with the covers up over his head. He tells me that if he gets up he is going to die. You had better get over here and help him get up." The harrassment of the Sales Manager was the final straw that broke the camel's back. It began with childhood but it points out the extreme fatigue that comes from mental harassment.

Fatigue Producing Emotions

The Bible tells us to love thy neighbor as thyself. The instruction used in so many wedding ceremonies from Ephesians 5:28, 29, says, "So ought men to love their wives as their own bodies. He that loveth his wife loveth himself. For no man ever yet hated his own flesh; but nourisheth and cherisheth it." The person who has never developed his own self-esteem, who does not respect himself, who does not have a strong self-image is either a character-void or extremely insecure individual who is especially prone to the mental harassment of others that brings about the conditions leading to tragic fatigue. Donald A. and Eleanor C. Laird in their book, *Tired Feelings and How to Master Them,* give us the following illustrations of situations which do the most damage to this sensitive inner self and touch off tired feelings. They are: "(1) Being ignored or neglected. (2) Being overshadowed. (3) Being interrupted or distracted. (4) Being jealous of the other person. (5) Simply disliking the person. (6) Being criticized or disparaged. (7) Being bossed or picked on. (8) Being nagged or preached at. (9) Being discriminated against. (10) Being bored by the other person."[4]

The story is told of the man in an office who constantly complained about his tired feet. When asked about it he explained that his shoes were too tight and his feet were killing him. The answer usually was, "Why don't you take off your shoes? We don't mind. Go without your shoes." And he would answer: "All day here at the office I take the criticism of my boss who doesn't like my work. Then when I get home at night, before I walk up the steps good, my big fat wife will start in criticizing me for not having brought home more pay. Then when I get in the house my mother-in-law will start telling me what's wrong with me and what a no-good son-in-law I am. Seated in the only comfortable chair in the living room will be my no-good brother-in-law who hasn't worked in thirty years. He bums off me all the time. Then my daughter will come in fussing about how life has failed her. She is the one who ran off and married a no-good character when she was still in high school and then he left her with three children. Before long they will run screaming through the house, demanding to know what there is for supper. The only thing I've got to look forward to tonight is taking my shoes off."

Young said, "An emotion is an acute disturbance of the individual as a whole, psychological in origin, involving behaviour, conscious experience, and visceral function."[5]

Man has two nervous systems. One is the central nervous

---

[4]Laird, Donald A. and Eleanor C., *Tired Feelings and How to Master Them* (New York: McGraw-Hill, 1960).
[5]Clark, *Ibid.*

system which is concerned mostly with adjustment between the external environment and the body. The other is the autonomic nervous system which has to do primarily with adjustments within the body. The autonomic system controls the visceral muscles, the glands, and the heart. The central system controls the skeletal muscles' and emotions. The autonomic system innovates virtually every internal organ of the body to a greater or lesser degree. In the exciting emotions like fear and anger it is the sympathetic division of this system which accelerates heart action, quickens breathing rate, raises blood pressure, stimulates the secretion of the adrenal gland, decreases or stops digestive activity, and so on. The pleasurable emotions arise as the result of the activity of the para-sympathetic division of the autonomic system. Most of the glands and the visceral muscles receive innovation from both of these two divisions of the autonomic system. An acute emotional disturbance can produce changes in our physical reaction. It is easy to understand how chronic emotional tensions may exert far reaching effects, influencing greatly the action of the heart, the secretion of the glands, the digestion, and other functions. It is certain that emotional behavior has both autonomic and bodily aspects.

Of course, emotions vary greatly. Some, like love, kindness, happiness, and sympathetic response are pleasurable. These contribute to the well-being of the organism. The others, like fear, anger and hate, tend to be harmful to our whole makeup.

Three Levels of Emotional Intensity

There are three levels of emotions distinguished by three degrees of intensity: (1) Weak or mild emotions which are all pleasant through stimuli may or may not be present. Anything that produces mild excitement that is pleasant, that is, the sight of good food, putting the finger in front of the revolving fan, coasting, or other acts of appreciation. (2) Strong emotions, which are characterized by bodily change in equilibrium amounting to a crisis. Such emotions are accompanied by a vivid feeling of pleasantness or unpleasantness. (3) Disrupted emotions which result in loss of coordination and mental upset. These emotions may be pleasant but frequently they are unpleasant. They result from states of frustration so great in intensity or are so unendurable in length as to make solution of the difficulty impossible. Such emotions are marked by trembling, paralysis, loss of control of bodily function, serious glandular disorders, and by hallucinations and delusions.

Let me urge you to get C. B. Eavey's book, *The Principles of Mental Health for Christian Living*, by Moody Press. You will find an outstanding development of the emotional effect upon our whole being.

These Problems Cause Fatigue

There are five basic problems that contribute to the psychological involvement of fatigue. They are:

(a) *Boredom.* Have you noticed how much more tired you are after you have spent an uneventful day with not much going on? Recently I spent nearly a day with my wife shopping, walking around a large department store, trying to pick out gifts for Christmas. Most of the time I was just waiting, standing around letting her make the decisions. Because of my unfamiliarity with the children's sizes of clothing and their specific needs and because of my abrupt decisiveness of action over against the slow deliberative manner my wife has in making a decision, I literally was bored. At the end of the day I was exhausted. Yet the carrying of the packages was not nearly as strenuous as walking eighteen holes of golf. It was boredom that made me tired.

The function of the nervous system is twofold, according

to Dr. David Harold Fink in his book, *Release From Nervous Tension*. "The nervous system is to keep us in contact with the world around us and to integrate our life activities. Integrate means to unify, to keep us all in one piece, to coordinate effort. The nervous system is our chief communication and coordinating center."[6]

So when a day has been spent in a manner that does not coordinate all of our efforts toward the achievement of our chief major purpose, then boredom has taken its toll for we feel this day was wasted.

Dr. Fink also says, "Emotion is hypnotic. Emotion prevents one from thinking clearly, from seeing sharply, from hearing accurately. It makes one blind, deaf, and dumb. It paralyzes activity that is just under your hand, keeps you from doing what you really want to do, and makes you do things that you would not do if you were in full possession of all of your faculties. How emotion can cut one off from even physical sensation is demonstrated by a football player who went through half a game with broken ribs, entirely unaware of the pain. Under emotional stress he enjoyed what amounts to hypnotic anesthesia that blocked his awareness of severe physical suffering."[7]

Hypnotizing Pain

On the kickoff of my first college football game in the fall of 1946 I was hit with a glancing block by a lineman who weighed fifty pounds more than I. Thrown through the air, I landed on my left shoulder, dislocating it. At the moment I suffered severe pain but after a few moments the pain subsided, and with the excitement of the game the pain was actually eliminated. During the half time rest it came again, but during the second half I forgot it. Upon being replaced by a substitute in the latter part of the fourth

[6]Fink, David Harold, *Relief From Nervous Tension* (New York: Simon and Schuster, 1943).
[7]*Op. cit.*

quarter, I was amazed to find my shoulder starting to hurt again. This injury resulted in my having to give up football, yet during the process of that game I literally felt no pain. The emotional intensity of playing the game had a hypnotic effect upon the pain, actually completely controlling it.

(b) *Worry* is the second major cause of psychological impact of fatigue. Worry, according to Marie Ray, is, "a mental tornado, a complete cycle of inefficient thought whirling around a pivot of fear. A dog chasing its own tail." Don't let worry make you so bone weary tired that you lose all function. Here are some ways to overcome worry: (1) Use your intelligence to see that worry is defeating the ends of your existence. (2) Substitute constructive thinking for circular feeling. (3) Change your emotional attitude toward whatever it is that is worrying you. (4) Develop a balanced life in which case worry can actually be wiped out.

Worry is a spasm of the emotions. The mind catches hold of something and will not let it go.

Winston Churchill has said, "It is useless to argue with the mind in the worrying condition. The stronger the will the more futile the task. One can only gently insulate something else into its convulsive grasp and if this something is rightly chosen, if it is really attended by the illumination of another field of interest, gradually, and often quite swiftly, the old grip relaxes and the process of recuperation and repair begin."

If you have any doubt as to the price worry pays listen to the quote of Dr. Clement G. Martin, author of, *How to Live to be 100,* published by Fell: "The facts are clear. The more sedentary the occupation the more dangerous it is. Three and a half times more deaths from hardening of the arteries occur among professional men than among unskilled laborers."

You Can Blow Your Stack

For example, high blood pressure can rise fifty points just from excitement. Yet a period of twenty minutes of controlled rest can drop a person's blood pressure by forty or fifty points. The tragedy is that the body, the innocent bystander, catches the free-for-all battle of conflicting emotions in the neck, in the small of the back, between the shoulder blades and even in the heart.

The Value of Relaxation

This truth is illustrated in the fact that a drunk involved in an automobile wreck is seldom hurt as seriously as the sober person. Why? The reason is simply this — the drunk has lost control of his emotions, isn't even aware he's about to have an accident and so his muscles are completely relaxed. The sober person tenses his muscles until they are hard as a rock. Then when they are brought into sudden impact with the automobile dashboard or thrown out into the street or whatever, these muscles, like hard rocks, are shattered or seriously injured.

I certainly don't recommend your getting drunk but I do recommend that you learn to relax your muscles through controlled activity.

(c) The feeling of *inferiority* results in psychological involvement and fatigue. Seventy-five per cent of all the college students enrolling for college and seventy-five per cent of the young people applying for jobs in America sell themselves short of their real ability. What is the cause of this tragic loss of manpower? These individuals do not believe in themselves. Their parents and other leaders have not developed true initiative, have not motivated them, have not led them to realize that they are important. We have over-emphasized the ego-maniac until we have discouraged the average person from actually giving his best. This frustration stops growth, sending the child or youth back to a level of adjustment suitable only to a lower age group.

There is nothing more destructive to a child's personality than to be told that he is just like the black sheep of the family. The divorced mother, who in anger turns to the child and says, "The reason you are no good is that you are just like your trifling dad." Such statements as this drive the child into tragic withdrawal and make the child regress to a lower stage of emotional and mental development.

Hate in War

One of the signs of feeling of inferiority is hate toward others. Earl Nightingale in one of his radio programs quotes Eric Hoffer, "It is easier to hate an enemy with much good in him than one who is all bad. We cannot hate those we despise.

"The Japanese had an advantage over us in World War II in that they admired us more than we admired them. They could hate us more fervently than we could hate them. The Americans are poor haters in International affairs because of their innate feeling of superiority over all foreigners. An American's hatred for a fellow American is far more virulent than any antipathy that he can work up against foreigners. It seems that when we are oppressed by the knowledge of our worthlessness we do not see ourselves as lower than some and higher than others, but as lower than the lowest of mankind. We hate then the whole world, and we would pour out our wrath upon the whole of creation."[8]

Then we would agree that intense hatred can suggest a strong feeling of inferiority. Five minutes of intensive hate burns more energy than eight hours of hard work. Now if you have boundless energy and can afford some delicious hates then you are the exception. Most of us have just so much energy. I would recommend that you use your energy

---

[8]*Our Changing World.*

for the attainment of your chief major goal — that you not dissipate your energies upon bitterness and strife and hatred. This inevitably leads to tragic fatigue.

(d) *Fear*. Fear first makes its blighting effect upon the individual by the rejection of the parent or of the older brother or sister. The child becomes harassed with the fear that he isn't wanted. The most important human emotion is tenderness. When the child is highly undervalued by the members of his own family, who above all others should accept him, how can he expect to value himself as he should? Early rejection by these who should love him the most tend to encourage self-rejection which leads to neurosis.

Fear is the immediate and instantaneous emotional reaction to those sensations which are strange and unexplainable to the individual. Fear is the most powerful of all the emotions. Cowles in his book, *Don't Be Afraid*, said, "When fear strikes on a particular series of mental images, their neurogram persists. . . . The mental images, the ideas, and the fear that was originally associated with them blaze immediately across your horizon, blinding you to everything else."9 (Editor's note: Neurogram is the system of measuring the nerve.)

Know Your Fears

Dr. Cowles says there are two separate kinds of fear: "There are normal fears such, for instance, as anyone experiences when he sees a ten ton truck bearing down on him. Under the impetus of such a normal fear, you sprint for safety and, standing clear of the truck, watch it pass while your fear gradually subsides into a state of thankfulness that you have escaped the wheels. But there are also pathological fears, and these are the fears we are talking about here. Normal fears help to maintain and prolong

9Cowles, Edward, *Don't Be Afraid* (New York: Wilcox and Fallett, 1941).

life by teaching us caution. Pathological fears are the form of disease. Though they seldom destroy life, they kill off all the pleasure one can have in being alive."[10]

Dr. David Harold Fink in his book, *Release From Nervous Tension*, says "Fifty years ago, William James said that 'you do not run because you fear; you fear because you run.' He was on the right track, for sensation follows organic reaction. So what is this emotion that we call fear? It is not a thing but a process, something that we do in five stages. First, we are conditioned both to proceed and fly from whatever we have learned to fear. Second, when a situation arises that we recognize as dangerous, we respond with our muscles by preparing for flight or escape. We tense up as a sprinter does when waiting for the signal go. Third, here is where feeling comes in because, as a result of muscular attitude preparatory to flight, there follow certain nervous and bodily changes. Fourth, some of your bodily responses stir up disagreeable sensations and feelings which you want to get rid of and which create fear and are secondary motives to find release in safety. Fifth, if for any reason you cannot run away and an appropriate action is frustrated, your emotion of fear may build up into paralyzing terror."[11]

While overseas in World War II I had the privilege of knowing an All-American end who is one of the most fearless men in combat I ever saw. Yet every time he was to get an injection he collapsed. He actually fainted. On Okinawa one day we were to receive three shots. As we walked through the tent of the medical corpsmen we received a shot in the right arm and the left arm at the same time and then a second shot in the right arm. This All-American football star fainted even before he got to the place to receive his shot.

Likewise, another college football player, a classmate of

[10]*Op. cit.*
[11]Fink, *Ibid.*

mine, was literally frightened out of his wits at the dark. He could not sleep in a room where there wasn't a light. He would call for someone else to walk with him down a flight of stairs in the night even though the stairs were lighted. Yet this man went on to attain a brilliant military record and is today a high ranking military officer headed for a generalship.

Fear Brings Fatigue

One man said, "I spend 75% of my time and energy doing my job and the other 25% making sure that someone else doesn't do me." This is an expression of fear that he will be replaced by someone else. We have today in business the throat cutting and backstabbing. This is just as fatigue-producing as the fear of physical injury or disease. It is a threat to the economic existence of the individual.

The case is clearly seen. Fatigue is primarily psychologically produced as the negative emotions produce their destructive way into our being. Our bodies are directly affected. Let us face up to these causes and proceed to learn to overcome them. There is nothing more destructive. You can make a habit of succeeding.

Some of the human responses to these frustrating situations in life are:

(a) *Reacting in kind* to the emotions received, that is, returning hostility to the individual who is hostile to us. I never cease to be amazed at the coolness and the calmness of the telephone operator. It has been a long time since I detected a telephone operator respond in hostility, and I have heard some men be very unkind to the operators when they couldn't get their number immediately. The Christian principle of turning the other cheek still works. If you can do this you are rapidly becoming a mature person.

(b) *Daydreaming* is another escape attitude that some people perform to fight their hostility. Now there is a differ-

ence in daydreaming and wishing. Wishing, in my defini-
tion, is the constructive manner of overcoming the problem
with a positive solution. Daydreaming is an escape mechanism that has no practical nor permanent accomplishment or
achievement. When you come down out of your clouds
you still have the same old problem to deal with. Running
from the problem will not solve it.

How to Be Happy

Dr. Heneage Ogilvie, the British surgeon and author of
the book, *No Miracles Among Friends,* has this to say, "we
make a great mistake if we think that happiness consists in
having a forty-hour week, a smart car, a television set, and
a chrome-plated bathroom.

"Happiness consists in (a) A job that provides a succession
of varied and interesting tasks. (b) That demands skill.
(c) And call for individual enterprise. (d) That is useful
to the community in which we live. (e) That offers security
if we do it conscientiously. (f) And advancement if we do
it well. (g) And if not a belief in a future life, at any rate
a confident belief in the future that this life holds for us. All
these things, the craftsmen and the peasants of the middle
ages had. All, or nearly all of them we lack today."[12]

This British surgeon has well summed up the fatigue
problem of the present day.

Now, if fatigue is the diminished capacity for doing work,
actual ability to work as well as the desire to work is cut
down. Someone else has said, "Fatigue is a temporary
decrease in efficiency resulting from work, play, or mental
action in any sort without rest."

Now let's define this problem of fatigue a little bit more.
What is the unconscious motivation behind it? What causes
us to act with our emotions as we so often do? Isn't it true
that we oftentimes act as we do in order to cover up for

[12]Laird, *Ibid.*

another weakness? Let's face the situation direct. If our boss is the problem; if he's constantly criticizing our work; if he is an autocratic leader who is never satisfied, then do one of several things: (1) Take the problem to him face to face. Tell him that you can't work under his tyranny. Ask him to transfer you somewhere else or leave you alone. (2) Look for different employment. Try to find more amiable working situations. (3) Isolate him and his conduct so he won't bother you. Dr. Andrew Potter of Oklahoma used to say, "You can't keep a donkey from braying but you can build a fence around him and shut the gate."

The day of the autocratic leader is rapidly passing away. Today the leadership is on a committee and suggestion basis primarily. However, some people are autocratic because they were trained in their home to be dictatorial. They may have a bit of paranoia, but as Dr. Lofton Hudson, one of America's outstanding counselors, said, "Don't knock the paranoids. They do three-fourths of the world's work." Your boss may be autocratic and tyrannical but sometimes men like this accomplish far more than those who are not inner motivated. The man of action has no use nor understanding for the individual of inaction. You are going to have to decide whether you are going to stay with a person who is doing things or leave. If you cannot isolate his tyranny in order to work with him, then you will have to leave, or if you cannot adjust to the situation to protect your own health and emotional happiness then you will have to leave.

Marie Ray in her book, *How Never to Be Tired*, gives the following important information, "From March to June, 1918, the British Army in France was constantly retreating. What happened? The hospitals were filled with men who suffered no physical injury, who were not wounded — who were merely exhausted. When the army began to advance again the number of those cases was tremendously reduced. Men on long marches dropped with physical fatigue but after a brief rest they went on again in good condition, few needing to be retired to the rear."[13] Unquestionably it was the emotional factor of losing — the sense of defeat — that drove them to the hospital with gross fatigue.

This Pig Had a Nervous Breakdown

Dr. Ray also tells about the pig that had a nervous breakdown. None ever did until March, 1937, when a pig named Achilles, a laboratory pig at Cornell University, was deliberately given a nervous breakdown by Dr. Howard Liddell, the phychiatrist of the college. The idea was to discover better ways to deal with nervous breakdowns in humans. How did Dr. Liddell proceed to give Achilles a nervous breakdown? By overworking him? By undernourishing him? By giving him drugs that tampered with his glands? No, by none of these methods. He simply worried him. For a year he gave Achilles one problem after another. He put an apple in the pen but made it increasingly more difficult for Achilles to get the apple. Worry drove him to a nervous breakdown.

The fatigue laboratory of Harvard University over a ten year study of this subject issued the following report of factory workers: (1) The fatigue of the factory worker cannot be defined in physiological terms, such as the amount of lactic acid, toxins, etc., present in the body. (2) That it is too subtle to yield to the physiologists' measurements such as pulse rate, blood pressure, etc. (3) That even the sensory test used by psychologists give no clear idea what it is and how it is brought on. (4) The phenomena formerly called fatigue is better described as boredom. It is boredom that caused a reduced rate of working.

In another test conducted in 1949 at Tufts College the experimenters found that worry, anger, indecision, indifference, unwillingness to apply, and lack of interest were the

---

[13]Ray, *Ibid.*

real causes of fatigue. The students who had gone without sleep for long periods, over a period actually of three sleepless days and nights, were not overcome by fatigue, but the students who had had emotional conflicts, worry, anger, indecision, etc., showed marked signs of fatigue.

Listen to the doctors and hear their story. Dr. Karl Menninger, author of *The Human Mind*, says, "Fifty per cent of those who go to doctors suffer from nervous rather than organic disorders. They represent the largest class of patients in clinics, dispensaries, and private practice."[14] Again Dr. Brill said, "Approximately 100% of the chronic fatigue of sedentary workers who are in good health is nervous fatigue."

Five Causes of Fatigue

"You will break the bow if you keep it always stretched," said Phaedrus. Causes of fatigue are many. Donald A. and Eleanor C. Laird in their book, *Tired Feelings and How to Master Them*, give us the following causes of fatigue: "(a) Overwork which runs down one's energy supply. (b) Diseases which exhaust, as in chronic infections, or interfere with, as with diabetes, the use of one's energy. (c) Bodily conditions which exhaust and interfere with the use of energy, such as, sedentary living, vitamin shortages, allergies, old age, overweight, high altitudes, and hot work places. (d) Personality clashes, off the job as well as on the job, which threaten the inner self and produce reactions that disrupt the use of energy. (e) Restricted situations, off the job as well as in one's work, which threaten the inner self and thereby produce attitudes that make it difficult to use one's energy."[15]

We see then that one of the main causes of fatigue, repeating itself over and over again, is the problem of emotional clashes. The individual who works at a mentally taxing

14*Our Changing World*, No. 843.
15Laird, *Ibid*.

situation where emotional conflicts are regularly involved and does not keep his physical body in a program of rigid fitness is far more likely to develop bone-crushing fatigue than the individual who works physically and does not involve himself with as many emotional and mental conflicts.

Man is a gregarious individual and wants to be loved and wants to love in return. When hostility, animosity, bitterness, hatred and strife enter into this climate of love, frustration and despair result. When an individual fails to reach the goals that he has inwardly established or when he is in a situation that will not allow him to reach his goals he is frustrated. Now if he has a regular program of physical fitness, of golf, of working in the yard, of exercise at the gym — anything that is deviational and physically exhausting — gives him an opportunity to dispel this despair and frustration in creativity.

My church has an activities building with a gymnasium and skating on the gym floor and volleyball and basketball, four bowling alleys — it even has a sauna room. When I regularly can work out there in the physical fitness program my creative mental production is greatly increased.

Your Success Checkup

1. What are the three kinds of fatigue?
2. What are the four signs of fatigue?
3. Donald L. Laird in the book, *Tired Feelings and How to Master Them,* lists ten causes of tired feelings. Restate them.
4. What are the five basic problems that contribute to fatigue?

6.
HOW TO FIGHT FATIGUE

A problem well-stated is half solved. Fear is wonderful if it brings about decided results for positive improvement. Fear is destructive if we wallow in the quagmire it brings. You must move on to a positive program of fighting fatigue.

Work

The diplomat and author, George F. Keenan, is quoted as saying, "If you ask me whether a country with no highly developed sense of national purpose, with the overwhelming accent of life on personal comfort, with the dearth of public services and surfeit of privately sold gadgetry, with insufficient social discipline has, over the long run, good chances of competing with a purposeful, serious and disciplined society such as that of the Soviet Union, I must say that the answer is no."[1]

This issue of national purpose as it relates itself to work is of vital concern to every free thinking man. *Life* magazine

[1]Levenstein, Aaron, *Why People Work* (New York: Crowell-Collier, 1964).

ran a series of articles on "The National Purpose." Such leading Americans as John K. Jessup, Adlai Stevenson, Archibald Macleish, David Sarnoff, Billy Graham, John W. Gardner, Clinton Rossiter, Albert Wohlstetter, James Reston and Walter Lippmann contributed articles to this study.

This decline of individual and national purpose is in my mind a direct result of what Dr. Sorokin, the outstanding sociologist of Harvard, calls "our sensate society." We are a nation of too much material possessions. Our children are lavishly given all they desire. Our government far too often gives its people what they want rather than what they need.

The immediate response to President John F. Kennedy's statement in his inaugural address on January 20, 1961, "Ask not what your country can do for you, but what you can do for your country," is an indication that thinking people are aroused at this concept of getting rather than the principle of giving.

In his book, *Why People Work*, Aaron Levenstein quotes David Riceman: "The change in the meaning of work is even plainer. For the inner directed person, work seemed self-justified; the only problem was to find the work to which one felt called. As we have seen, the age of expanding frontiers provided the individual with an inexhaustible list of tasks. Work, like property, moreover, was considered a mode of relating oneself to physical objects, and only indirectly to people. Indeed, the work hungry inner directed types of this period sometimes found that they were cut off from family and friends, and often from humanity in general, by their assiduity and diligence. And work, like property, was a defense against psychological invasion, a 'Do not disturb' sign, guarding the industrious man of the middle class.

"Today the meaning of work is a very different one, psychologically, though in many professions and industries the older mode still persists. To an increasing degree, the self is no longer defined by its productive accomplishments but by its role in a 'friendship' system."[2]

Work That Excites

The individual who gets up in the morning excited about his work, who believes that he is making a definite contribution to his community, to his family, to his work associates, to the people that he serves through his employment, to God and to his country, isn't bothered by fatigue. Here is a man who reflects an inner glory of conviction.

Seldom have I agreed with Bertrand Russell, but in this quote I do: "Those who live nobly, even if in their day they live obscurely, need not fear that they will have lived in vain. Something radiates from their lives, some light that shows the way to their friends, their neighbors, perhaps to long future ages. I find many men nowadays oppressed with a sense of impotence, with a feeling that in the vastness of modern society there is nothing of importance that the individual can do. This is a mistake. The individual, if he is filled with the love of mankind, with breadth of vision, with courage and endurance, can do a great deal."[3] Work is the sustained activity to which a man commits his most productive hours, talents, and mental power, as a burning conviction that life is worth living.

Dr. Erich Fromm believes that present day industrialism in both the capitalist and the communistic world is reducing the individual to a "well-fed and well-entertained automaton, who loses his individuality, his independence and his humanity." However, this need not be so. If we will practice the principles of motivation that James F. Lincoln of Lincoln Electric Company has used in increasing the productivity of his employees to a fantastic degree, then we will make work a magnificent obsession. Mr. Lincoln has his factory

---

[2]Levenstein, Aaron, *Ibid.*
[3]Edwards, Tyron, *The New Dictionary of Thoughts* (New York: Standard Book Co., 1955).

employees on a piece work basis. They are paid according to their individual productivity. Then he has developed a team spirit, the old high school athletic "gung ho" concept of total commitment to a group identification. Here the individual feels an identity with others, but also is able to assert himself as a free man in a free society challenged to give his best.

I've found no greater contrast in the attitudes toward work than in these following quotes: Thomas Carlyle: "All Work, even cotton spinning, is noble; work alone is noble — a life of ease is not for any man, nor for any god. Even in the meanest of sorts of labors, the whole soul of man is composed into a kind of real harmony the instant he sets himself to work. Blessed is he who has found his work; let him ask for no other blessedness." The contrasting attitude is reflected in a chant of the industrial workers of the world, "We go to work to get the dough to get the food to get the strength to go to work to get the dough, to get the food."

Throughout the Judaeo Christian tradition we have the dignity of work. The modern union movement was a definite result of the Welsh revivals. It is quite interesting that the Hebrews revealed their attitude for work by using the same terms, *Avodah*, for both work and worship.

Results Expected

In the Bible in Matthew 25:14-30 there is the parable of the talents when the master expected his servants each to be faithful according to his several abilities. Notice the two who were both faithful but had different abilities, different talents, for they were rewarded the same. The unjust servant had his reward taken from him and given to the one who was faithful.

Robert Blauner in his book, *Work Satisfaction and Industrial Trends in Modern Society*, states that there are three basic factors that account for vocational satisfaction. One is occupational prestige — the community's attitude toward the work of this particular vocation. For example, even though the factory worker is frequently higher paid than the office worker, office workers are given higher social prestige. Two — the degree of control over his work that the individual feels he has. If he has the ability to make and the liberty to make decisions about his work, he enjoys it more. Three — the degree of integration with his work group that the individual feels.

How to Enjoy Your Work

Voltaire said, "Work keeps at bay three great evils: boredom, vice, and need." Dale Carnegie gives good advice, "By thinking the right thoughts, you can make any job less distasteful. Your boss wants you to be interested in your job so that he will make more money. But let's forget about what the boss wants. Think only of what getting interested in your job will do for you. Remind yourself that it may double the amount of happiness you get out of life, for you spend about one half of your waking hours at your work, and if you don't find happiness in your work, you may never find it anywhere. Keep reminding yourself that getting interested in your job will take your mind off your troubles, and in the long run, will probably bring promotion and increased pay. Even if it doesn't do that, it will reduce fatigue to a minimum and help you enjoy your hours of leisure."[4] Here we have the quote of one of the world's outstanding motivators on how work will overcome and diminish fatigue. Remember, your mind is the only thing in this world you totally control. So give yourself a pep talk about the positive results of your work and you will find life really worth living.

When has there been among us an individual more motivated by his work than Dr. Thomas Dooley, the St. Louis

---
[4]Carnegie, *Ibid.*

physician who challenged the altruistic concern of all peoples everywhere by the establishment of his hospitals in Southeast Asia? Although cancer took this dedicated and outstanding young humanitarian he made, in the short period of a few years, an immortal impact upon society as he pricked the conscience of the Christian world with his work toward easing the hurt of humanity.

Helen Keller said, "Look where we will, we find the hand in time and history, working, building, inventing, bringing civilization out of barbarism." The hand symbolized power and the excellence of work. The mechanic's hand that ministers elemental forces, the hand that hews, saws, cuts, builds, is useful in the world equally with the delicate hand that paints a wild flower or molds a Grecian urn, or the hand of a statesman that writes a law. The eye cannot say to the hand, "I have no need of thee." Blessed be the hand. Thrice blessed be the hands that work.

Calvin Coolidge relates our work with our mental and spiritual growth. "All growth depends upon activity. There is no development physically or intellectually without effort, and effort means work. Work is meaningful; it is the prerogative of intelligence, the only means to manhood and the measure of civilization." And Kahlil Gibrian said, "If you cannot work with love but only with distaste it is better that you should leave your work and sit at the gate of the temple and take alms of those who work with joy."

Charles Evans Hughes declared, "I know hardly anyone who works too hard. I believe in hard work and long hours of work. Men do not break down from overwork but from worry and from plunging into dissipation and efforts not aligned with their work." Theodore Roosevelt said, "I don't pity any man who does hard work worth doing. I admire him. I pity the creature who doesn't work at whichever end of the social scale he may regard himself as being."

Work Is an Investment

Please realize that the persistency and diligence in your work will inevitably bring achievement and success. William James states this principle: "Let no youth have any anxiety about the upshot of his education whatever the line of it may be. If he keeps faithfully busy each hour of the working day, he may safely leave the final result to itself. He can, with perfect certainty, count on waking up some fine morning to find himself one of the confident ones of his generation, in whatever pursuit he may have singled out." And Dale Carnegie has so well stated the dilemma of vast multitudes of people when he said, "A shockingly large number of our worries and our hidden tensions stem from the fact that millions of people have never found themselves, have never discovered the kind of work they could love and do well. Instead they seethe with inner rebellion because they spend their lives doing work they despise." My friend, if you don't like your work, if your work doesn't contribute to others, to your country, to God, to your family and to your own inner satisfaction, then change jobs. Find something you feel is challenging and idealistic and is making a contribution to others' lives. Lowell Thomas has suggested, "Do a little more each day than you think you possibly can." This is how you exceed. This is how you excel. This is how the first four minute mile was achieved. The runner paced himself a little more each day than he did the day before. This is how any achievement is attained and this is the way to fight fatigue.

Attitude and Purpose

So by changing your attitude toward your work and making it a wonderfully exciting experience you accomplish two purposes. (1) You overcome emotional fatigue. Oh, certainly, you may be physically tired — more than you were before. But, remember, rest, recreation and good food overcome physical fatigue. In fact, physical fatigue is fine. It gives the sense of satisfaction at the end of the day that we really have exerted ourselves. (2) You find a new purpose for your life. Life will take on new meaning. You will get up in the morning excited about the day's opportunities. And you will return home at night excited because you have realized that the greatest use of life is to so live your life that the usefulness of your life will outlive you. You have given yourself to a cause greater than yourself, and you have left a lasting impression and influence for others. This truly is cultivating the habit of succeeding.

Use These Weapons in the Battle Against Fatigue

(1) *Practice positive thoughts.* Thomas Carlyle has said, "Silence is the element in which great things fashion themselves. Native bearers on Safari in Africa will not travel on the seventh day. They didn't get this conviction from Biblical training. However it has come from spiritual insight. The reason they simply will not travel on the seventh day is in their words, 'Our souls must catch up with our bodies.'"

You literally can change your life by scheduling a period every day of silent meditation. Just fifteen minutes a day will reflect marvelous changes in your life. During this period saturate your pause and very being with positive thoughts. Remember, the only principle that all philosophers of all ages have agreed upon is this, "As a man thinketh in his heart, so is he." We become what we think about. Marcus Aurelius more than eighteen hundred years ago said, "Our life is what our thoughts make it."

One of the fallacies of our day is the statement, "You can't change human nature." This is untrue. Human nature can be changed in the following formula:

(1) Facing the fact of our disobedience to the laws of God which inevitably bring on severe guilt complexes and

result in negative thoughts, negative emotions, and negative reactions.

(2) By faith in God our lives can be literally remade.

(3) Through the action of personal faith; through the conduct of unselfish service to others, man can literally be changed in his life.

In one of his radio addresses Earl Nightingale quotes John Stewart Mill, "He who lets the world, or his own portion of it, choose his plan of life for him, has no need of any other faculty than the ape-like one of imitation. He who chooses his plan for himself, employs all his faculties. He must use his observation to see, reasoning and judgment to foresee, activity to gather materials for decision, discrimination to decide, and when he has decided, firmness in self-control to hold to his deliberate decision.

"Human nature is not a machine to be built after a model and set to do exactly the work prescribed for it, but a tree, which requires to grow and develop itself on all sides, according to the tendency of the inward forces that make it a living thing."

The Key to Growth

Now that's the key! Our life is like a tree that, nurtured by the water of positive thoughts, invigorated by the fertilizer of constructive action, cradled in the warm climate of fellowship, happy family and business relationships, assures sustained and proper growth in all directions.

Dale Carnegie has said, "Let's not waste a second worrying because we are not like other people. You are something new in this world. Never before, since the beginning of time, has there ever been anybody exactly like you; and never again throughout all the ages to come will there be anybody exactly like you again." And Carnegie also said, "If half a century of living has taught me anything at all, it has taught me that nothing can bring you peace but yourself."

Happiness comes from within and happiness can be controlled and expended and expanded. Remember, the only thing in this whole world you totally control is your own mind.

You see, the key to it all is attitude. Attitude means "position, disposition, or manner with regard to a person or thing." William James said, "It is our attitude at the beginning of a difficult task which, more than anything else, will affect its successful outcome."

Negative Destruction

Andrew Carnegie brought from Germany one of the world's outstanding steel experts to join the Carnegie Master Mind Group. This German expert had only been here a few months before his negative, cynical, critical attitude was a destructive and disharmonious element in the Steel Master Mind Alliance. At a considerable expense Mr. Carnegie paid off the German expert and sent him back to Europe. One negative thought can undermine an entire fellowship of positive minded individuals.

Following the teachings of Napoleon Hill on the Master Mind Alliance I organized such a group to bring industry, jobs and financial remuneration to the area where we lived, as well as to the individuals involved. Within a year's time this group was at the point of dissolvement and demanded total reorganization because of the negative mindedness of a few members of it, primarily of one person. Practically every constructive, creative thought that came forth from individuals in conference would be undermined by this negative minded individual.

So it is with you and your life. You may be positive to many expressions of your daily conduct, but if there's only one area that you are negative in then it will undermine all the rest of your personality and program of achievement.

Henry Chester said, "Faith and initiative rightly com-

bined remove mountainous barriers and achieve the un-
heard of and miraculous. An enthusiastic attitude is nothing
more than faith in action."

Get Interested in Your Job

Calvin Coolidge has said, "I have found it advisable not
to give too much heed to what people say when I am trying
to accomplish something of consequence. Invariably they
proclaim, 'It can't be done.' I deem that the very best time
to make the effort." Sir Ernest Shackleton declared, "I never
undertook anything of any measure in my life but what I
was told that my effort would end in futility. This once
caused me considerable worry. I no longer give it any
heed."

How to Change Your Life

Earl Nightingale, in his program, No. 625, tells the story
of two men — one who has received fabulous success as a
result of positive thoughts; the other who let his thoughts
ruin him. Both men were about the same age, both were
badly crippled by rheumatic fever, arms, legs, hands all
twisted terribly. One felt sorry for himself and this negative
thinking ruined his life. He became a tragic invalid, a
physical and financial and emotional burden on his family,
living an unhappy, unproductive life for more than thirty
years and bringing negative dissatisfaction to everyone he
touched. The other young man, whose mother made eight
dollars a week as a weaver, had just as great difficulties. He
graduated from high school, but rheumatic fever cut him
down before he was able to go to college and major in
chemistry. When he wasn't in a wheel chair he had to be
carried about like a baby. For five terrible years pain
racked his body. Then one day a magic thought entered his
mind. He said to himself, "How can I, crippled and chained
to a wheel chair, be of use to others?" Then the power of

his subconscious mind, his creative mind, began to work amazing, magical formulas of solution. He began by coloring post cards but the pay was inadequate. Then he worked out a plan to buy finished post cards and sell them by mail. Soon he was selling thousands of them. Now he has a million dollar business with a beautiful home in Massachusetts and another in Florida. The pilot of his private plane flies him all over the country. He has many hobbies and even plays the electric organ. This man's fabulous success started the day he quit worrying and feeling sorry for himself and started a mental attitude of positive thought. You literally can change your life by changing your attitudes of mind.

(2) *Sleep.* One of your major weapons of battling fatigue is sleep. Dr. Clement G. Martin, author of, *How to Live to Be a 100,* published by Fell says, "Sleep is a necessity of life, not a luxury. Too little sleep can result in the symptoms of a starvation even more dramatic than the symptoms caused by fasting from food. If sleeplessness is attempted for any prolonged period, our bodies will fail in one way or another."

Dr. Martin reminds us of the short sleeping hours of well-known people like Churchill, Edison and Napoleon. But what many people didn't realize is that through catnaps these same individuals would probably average six to eight hours in a twenty-four hour period.

How to Induce Sleep

Many years ago I took professional training in hypnosis, not only to use in counseling but also to use primarily for my own relaxation. When I find myself tired with many pressures and responsibilities I take out a few moments, either lie on the couch or on the floor or even in a comfortable chair, close my eyes and put myself into hypnotic trance. There are several key words I use that are most effective. The first word I use is *relax.* I say it over and over and over to relax my physical muscles. Then I repeat the word *peace* to relax my nerves. Then I repeat the word *heavy* and I imagine myself literally going through the chair or sofa, through the floor and into the ground. Then I repeat the word *feather* and I can imagine myself floating like a feather in the wind, on a cloud and in just a very few moments I can be under. I will tell myself how long I want to rest, whether it's five minutes or fifteen minutes and at that time I awaken tremendously refreshed. I have found that ten minutes of good rest like that in the middle of the day, breaking the tensions of the day, can actually mean as much or more to me than an extra hour of sleep at night.

Dr. David Harold Fink in his book, *Release From Nervous Tension,* gives a fine formula for a catnap. He says that a person should provide himself with a quiet, darkened room, with a bed and four small pillows, and a warm light blanket. He should undress or loosen his clothing so that there is no hampering his breathing. Then get into bed and arrange the pillows in the following manner. Pull one pillow down under the neck and the head rolls back toward the head of the bed. Be sure that the head and neck are perfectly comfortable. Then place the second pillow under the knees so that they are bent slightly and upward. This takes the tension off the large muscles back of the thigh. The knees should be bent and the legs spread so that the weight of the legs will be felt on the outside of the calf of the legs. Then the two other pillows are placed upon either side of the chest. Lay your arms upon them so that your elbows are about eight inches from the body. Then bend the elbow so that your wrists are close to your body. Now you are in the most conducive position for relaxation. Use this pattern regularly. Relax your jaw and tongue. Close your eyes. Just let go. Speak soothing words of relaxation to yourself. Talk to your arms, to your muscles and tell them to relax.

Repeat it over and over and over and over again. This is hypnotic.

Prime Minister Winston Churchill reported in his autobiography that he always took time out to relax. President Woodrow Wilson would give himself a relaxation break for fifteen minutes in the middle of every morning.

One of the most indefatigable individuals in American life today is Bob Hope. In a recent newspaper article entitled, *My Secret Weapon Against Fatigue,* Hope tells how he has been able to carry on the fabulous program he has had, and he is now in his early sixties. Bob Hope tells about how he relaxes on a busy plane. He pulls his hat down over his eyes. He wears a pair of wrap around isinglass dark glasses that completely shut out the light. Putting his feet up where they can be comfortable, he tries to relax for a catnap every day after lunch on the suggestion of his doctor. Furthermore, Bob Hope says that he almost never takes any kind of sleep inducing medication. He has made a habit out of catnaps and it literally has extended his life.

You, too, can change your life and fight fatigue effectively with a regular bombardment of catnaps.

(3) *Use these weapons in the battle against fatigue.* "I must lose myself in action lest I wither in despair," wrote Alfred Tennyson. A dynamic purpose drives away despair. Of course, purpose must be controlled. There are such individuals as "work addicts," people who with an inner uncontrollable compulsion must work. There are some rare individuals who overdo it. These are not in wise emotional balance. But they are the rare exceptions. You are not one of them.

A Formula to Fight Fatigue

Dr. Fink in his book suggests the following formulas on how to fight fatigue with purpose: (1) Learn to relax. Do it in your spare time. Carry your habits of relaxation over into your work. (2) Go easy on yourself. Bite off only as much as you can chew easily. Learn to do one thing well before you attempt a dozen other things. (3) Do anything in which you are or used to be interested. In other words rekindle the flame of a previous activity and make it a constructive tool in fighting fatigue — certainly an activity that brings pleasure and satisfaction and happiness and a sense of achievement.

Dale Carnegie has said, "I honestly believe that this is one of the greatest secrets to true peace of mind — a decent sense of values. And I believe we could annihilate fifty per cent of all our worries at once if we would develop a sort of private gold standard — a gold standard of what things are worth to us in terms of our lives." Remember, the inner directed individual who is consoled by his own character convictions, who does what he believes is right according to the teachings of the Bible — that individual can find true happiness because his purpose is controlled by higher law. The individual who simply is a will of the wisp, that is blown by the diversified hot or cold winds of outward direction, is a victim of the society he runs with. He has no high purpose.

Clean Windows

George Bernard Shaw said, "You cannot believe in honor until you have achieved it. Better keep yourself clean and bright; you are the window through which you must see the world." Henry Clay declared, "Sirs, I would rather be right than be President." And David Starr Jordan said, "The world stands aside to let anyone pass who knows where he is going." Theodore Roosevelt once said, "We have got but one life here. It pays, no matter what comes after it, to try and do things, to accomplish things in this life, and not merely to have a soft and pleasant time." Dale Carnegie points out, "If you want to be happy set yourself a goal that commands your thoughts, liberates your energy, and inspires your hopes. Happiness is within you. It comes from doing some certain thing into which you can put all your thought and energy. If you want to be happy, get enthusiastic about something outside yourself." Ralph Waldo Emerson declared, "Insist on yourself; never imitate. Your own gift you can present every moment with a cumulative force of a whole life cultivation; but of the adopted talent of another, you have only an extemporaneous half possession. That which each can do best none but his Maker can teach him." Henry David Thoreau said, "Public opinion is a weak tyrant, compared with our private opinion. When a man thinks of himself, that it is which determines, or rather indicates, his fate."

He Turned on a New Attitude

Let me illustrate for you what purpose does to fatigue. For years Joe had been planning to open his own business but he lacked one thing — money for capitalization. He had tried several get rich schemes and had lost money in each venture. Because of the sudden death of the president of his company, financial reverses had set in and he had not received the raises he had anticipated. Furthermore, his wife's lengthy illness with extensive hospitalization got him further into debt. All of this was deeply depressive. Joe became more and more saturated with fatigue. His mind was spouting negative weeds.

Then one day out of seemingly nowhere the answer came. Joe returned home one afternoon to find a registered letter from an unknown law firm. A distant uncle had died and left Joe ten thousand ($10,000) dollars. It was exactly the amount of money he needed. Joe quickly became a dynamic, purposeful, enthusiastic, excited individual. His mind now began to produce positive thoughts of beautiful flowers. His work took on new vigor to the extent that the new boss offered him a considerable raise. His wife's health actually improved. Joe became saturated with a desire to open up his business. He could hardly wait. His whole life had changed. Purpose had driven away fatigue.

Marie Ray, in her book, *How Never to Be Tired,* quotes the psychiatrist Adler, "There is no liability for which there is not a compensating asset, and that those who are severely handicapped often make their deficiencies the stepping stones to success. They over-compensate for their deficiency and in so doing develop qualities they would otherwise have lacked." Adler investigated the lives of famous painters and found that a large portion of them suffered from imperfections of sight. In the endeavor to make up for this early deficiency they trained themselves to use their eyes more carefully than most people with normal sight and so developed their visual sensitivity which is one of the artist's chief qualities.

Springboard to Success

A handicap can be a springboard to success. Almost always it is as much some inferiority in us as any special superiority we may possess that accounts for our success. There is nothing like an inferiority complex to bring out the best in us.

"That is why a one-legged girl like Louise Baker learns to ski; a blind man like Alec Templeton becomes a famous pianist; a man with a stammer and lisp like Churchill becomes a magnificent orator; a cockney girl like Gertrude Lawrence becomes the first lady of the stage; a one-legged man like peg-leg Bates learns to tap dance; a basket case like Charles Zimmy captures the world's distance and endurance swimming record by swimming a hundred and forty-five miles in one hundred forty-nine hours; an armless man like Dr. George B. Sutton, with no artificial attachments, becomes the billiard champion of two continents. All are over-compensating for an inferiority."[5]

Therefore, we can conclude that positive thoughts, a definite program of sleep, particularly daytime catnaps, and dynamic purpose are the chief weapons in the battle against fatigue.

Practice These Habits and Overcome Fatigue

William James has said, "The greatest discovery of my generation is that a man can alter his life by altering his attitudes of mind." If you have been one of these individuals who has been negative-minded all of your life and pessimistic about everything and have let your emotional problems harass and control you and literally drive you to a feeling of physical exhaustion, then, my friends, you must re-educate yourself if you are ever going to be an emotionally mature and physically healthy individual.

More than eighteen hundred years ago Marcus Aurelius said, "Our lives are what our thoughts make us." Let me urge you to restructure your entire life through a program of mental re-education.

Dr. Marie Ray gives this formula for your re-education plan: "(1) Learn how to overcome the devitalizing emotions. (2) Learn how to summon up the vitalizing emotions. For each emotional poison there is an emotional antidote. (3) Acquire a better philosophy of life. The new goals this sets for our efforts release healthier emotions. (4) Learn the law of compensation — that for every liability there exists a compensation. Learn how to overcome our psychological handicaps. (5) Learn that the ways to establish new ways of feeling and acting is through new habits. (6) Learn that the best way to balance our emotions is to balance our lives. Learn what is meant by a balanced life — and to lead it."[6]

[5]Ray, *Ibid.*
[6]*Op. cit.*

There is but one element essential for the entire changing of your life — courage. Francis Parkman throughout his life suffered from so many assorted sorts of pain that he could work only a few minutes at a stretch. Yet he produced two dozen large volumes of history. Milton was blind but he wrote *Paradise Lost*. Stevenson's body was wracked with tuberculosis yet he wrote some of the greatest adventure stories of our day. Gauguin gave up wealth and family to paint in loneliness and poverty. Pasteur was partially paralyzed but he carried on his uncompromising war with disease. Florence Nightingale carried on her mercy to the hurt of humanity from her sick bed and William Wilberforce was a man short of stature with a sickly body and little physical stamina, but he carried on a continuous war with opium, and by his moral courage led a worldwide battle against the slave trade and won. Boswell is quoted about Wilberforce, "I saw what seemed a mere shrimp mounted upon the table; but as I listened he grew and grew until the shrimp became a whale."

Thirteen Steps to an Energetic Life

Try this formula for creating better attitudes and overcoming fatigue: (1) Take charge of your mind. Strongly control hostile attitudes and negative emotions. Don't let fear and frustration and mental harassment bother you. (2) Plan to take a long period of time to create this climate. Set aside fifteen minutes every day that you will spend in giving yourself a pep talk. Expect your reconstruction period to last from six months to a year and let nothing deter you from accomplishing it. (3) Seek to improve the working conditions where you are. Some things you can accomplish yourself. If there is improper lighting and the company won't provide more, then get another desk lamp at your own expense if necessary. Try to work more cooperatively with your supervisor and with your co-workers. Remember, other people return to us the same attitudes we give unto them. Practice the golden rule and you will find it works. (4) Don't expect never to be tired again. Physical tiredness is a part of living and regardless of how well you reconstruct your life there will be certain periods when you are under special tension and strain from your work, when you will have emotionally induced tiredness. But if these come only at certain times then you can live with them. The real problem is when they are a daily part of our lives.

(5) After you have reconstructed your emotional life to a healthy-mindedness and if later, even years from now, you find yourself going through a period of sustained tiredness, remember that it may be the result of an organic problem. Go to your doctor and get a physical checkup to be sure you do not have a physical difficulty. Overweight people tend to be fatigued more than people who are not overweight. A doctor told me recently that the person that is 10% overweight has taken the best years off his life. Furthermore, he is hauling around that excessive load. The man that is forty pounds overweight is carrying a forty pound load on his back. But the trouble is, it isn't on his back! (6) Through our rest habits we contribute to our fatigue. Practice getting a good night's sleep. Learn to trust your subconscious mind by telling all your problems to this creative mind to solve them while you are resting. (7) Learn to relax your muscles and you will be able to overcome fatigue. Stan Musial, a former neighbor of mine in St. Louis Hills, always went through strenuous shoulder exercises before he batted. The idea was to release the tension of the heavy muscles, the shoulder muscles leading to the neck. He says this is the most important muscle and if it was tense it affected his swing. Learn how to work relaxed. I remember seeing All American football player, Doak Walker, star at SMU and of the Detroit Lions, return from a long pass to go back to the huddle totally relaxed. Then the moment the ball was

centered his every muscle was tensed to the totality of his ability. When the play was over he was totally relaxed again. Natural athletes learn how to relax their muscles. (8) Plan your program in such an organized manner that you will allow no time for boredom. If you don't have enough work then ask for more, or take books along to read when you've finished an assigned task. Time passes much faster when you are energetically at work.

(9) Learn to control your drive and you will be able to overcome fatigue. The intensely ambitious individual who is never satisfied with his achievements is far more prone to be a victim of fatigue than the person who can recognize his own achievement and have periods of satisfaction, realizing that an uncontrollable burning desire can be destructive to his health. (10) Develop some strong personal relationships with individuals you love and admire, people you like to be around. Don't let yourself be a wallflower. Associate with other individuals. Remember, we draw strength from the crowd we run with. In fact, we become what the crowd we run with is. Our fatigue can be easily dissipated through the association of warmhearted friends. (11) Disassociate yourself as much as you humanly can from the people that you dislike or the people who dislike you. It is emotionally destructive to be a part of a conflicting arrangement. Of course, the more numerous your personal problems are, then the more likely you are to be involved with fatigue. Settle your problems. Don't let them continue to harass you. (12) Learn to be effective in making decisions. Don't procrastinate. The more you postpone action the more the indecision harasses you and brings about fatigue. (13) Associate yourself with both subordinates and superiors who are enjoyable to work with. In other words, there will be far more fatigue when you are related to the dictator type person. The boss that will let you help plan your program,

outline your work, and then encourage you toward the performance of it is well worth staying with.

Another habit that will help you overcome fatigue is what I call the habit of excitement. Look for and anticipate some new excitative experiences in every day's normal activity. Realize that in every experience there is something new you can learn. With every new person you meet there is some value you will receive. Your whole life will expand and you will look forward to each day expecting excitingly different, new experiences to be yours.

Another good habit to form in overcoming fatigue is the attitude of play toward all that we do. Play is anything that we enjoy doing, that amuses and excites us. Now when children get tired of something they may drop it and go to something else. My work is so wonderfully diversified that when I get a bit tired of one thing I can shift and go to something else, and later when I feel refreshed I can come back to the first thing. This way there is a new fresh and exciting atmosphere about it all.

The individual who can't find the play attitude in his work is a neurotic and does not think he should have any fun in life. What a tragic attitude. This probably goes back to childhood when the child was forced to work and taught by the parents that all play or even any play is bad. Such individuals are work addicts. They are victimized by their background and never enjoy life. I tell you life is to be enjoyed. Life is to be lived to the fullest and the person who has the play attitude about his work never dreads his work but enjoys it immensely.

One of the most important habits you can form to overcome fatigue is the habit of a positive attitude. Just as the athlete develops habits that become the pattern of his athletic conduct, so we must develop habits that become the pattern, the form of our life. Remember, we can change our lives by changing our attitudes of mind. If it means you have to resign your job, move your family a thousand miles away and take up an entirely different vocation, do it if you must in order to form new attitudes. I think there is a tendency to get in a rut the longer we stay at a certain job in a certain vocation and a certain area. The freshness of moving to a new city, taking on new work, sometimes even a new type of work, even a new vocation brings excitement and new attitudes of life. This is why a baseball player is oftentimes traded when he has a bad year. Then the next year he may make a comeback that is fabulous and fantastic. His attitude changed once he changed ball clubs. You can change your life by changing your attitudes of mind.

In his book, *How to Live 365 Days a Year,* Dr. Schindler gives us twelve important principles of how to make our lives richer: "(1) Keep life simple. (2) Avoid watching for a knock in your motor. (3) Learn to like work. (4) Have a good hobby. (5) Learn to be satisfied. (6) Like people and join the human enterprise. (7) Get the habit of saying the cheerful, pleasant thing. (8) Meet adversity by turning defeat into victory. (9) Meet your problems with decision. (10) Make the present moment an emotional success. (11) Always be planning something. (12) Don't let irritating things get your goat."[7]

Satisfy These Six Needs

Realize that you have six basic needs and plan a program to satisfy these six basic needs and then, my friend, you will form the habit of overcoming fatigue. (1) *The need for love.* Everyone needs to give love and everyone needs to be loved. Find in your family, in the romance of your job, in your associates at work, in your social and church ac-

[7]Schindler, John A., *How to Live 365 Days a Year* (Englewood Cliffs, New Jersey: Prentice-Hall, Inc., 1955).

tivities this sense of belonging, the sense of service, and you will go a long way toward satisfying this need. (2) *The need to feel secure.* You should find in your faith the sense of spiritual security. You should find in the achievement of your job, knowing that the man who excels will never be without work, a sense of economic security. But, of course, a definite savings program and a fine insurance program will give you another sense of economic security. You will find in your family the sense of family and emotional security. You will find in the creativity of your achievement and success in your field of service a sense of people security — you are living for a cause greater than yourself. (3) *The desire to be creative.* Realize that your mind has unlimited resources. You can find the creative answer to whatever problem confronts you. (4) *The need for recognition.* Build a better mousetrap by outstanding achievement and you will be recognized by all men everywhere. (5) *The desire for new, fresh and exciting experiences.* You can find them in every day. (6) *Self-satisfaction, self-achievement.* This will come as you give of yourself unstintingly to your work. You will find a sense of achievement.

One other habit to form and you will overcome fatigue — that is the habit of a new start. Put everything behind you and start over again. Remember, you can learn from every experience. Some of the most outstanding individuals in this world were failures at an early age. They learned many ways how not to do a thing. Then they profited from their experience. Live in what Norman Vincent Peale calls daytight compartments. The Bible says, "Sufficient unto the day is the evil thereof." In other words, there are enough problems for each day without bringing yesterday's into today.

Remember, that with every morning you are given a new book — clean, unspoiled pages. And you are going to write into that book what you are that day and what you've done that day. Every day is fresh; every day is new. Start off with a fresh start every day.

Let every new day, new week, new month, new year give you a fresh start. Put the old things behind you. Recall only those past experiences that you need· for wisdom and for inspiration. Remember, the human mind has fantastic ability to forget and to remember. Crowd out of your mind those destructive things. Bring to the focus of your mind only those good things and you will make a habit of succeeding.

Your Success Checkup

1. What are the three basic factors that account for vocational satisfaction?
2. What is the three-step formula Dr. David Fink gives us in his book, *Release from Nervous Tension*, on how to fight fatigue?
3. What are the thirteen steps to an energetic life?
4. List the twelve important principles on "How to Make Your Life Richer" by Dr. Schindler.
5. List the six basic needs of each individual.

7.
ENERGY

How to Be an Energetic Person

Energy is the capacity for doing work. It means vigorous activity, the ability to produce action, vigor of expression, to exert power. Buxton says, "The longer I live, the more deeply am I convinced that that which makes the difference between one man and another — between the weak and the powerful, the great and the insignificant, is energy — invisible determination — a purpose once formed, and then death or victory. This quality will do anything that is to be done in the world and no talents, no circumstances, no opportunities will make one a man without it."[1] Goethe said, "Energy will do anything that can be done in this world; and no talents, no circumstances, no opportunities will make a two-legged animal a man without it." And Napoleon said, "The truest wisdom, in general, is a resolute determination." D. G. Mitchell declared, "There is no genius in life like the genius of energy and activity."

[1]Bogardus, *Ibid.*

What Is Energy?

There are two types of energy. (1) *Potential Energy*. Potential energy does not mean that energy is not real; this means that energy is stored away in some latent manner but can be drawn upon at will for the accomplishment of a particular action. (2) *Kinetic Energy*. This is the energy of motion — this is action. Energy is the sheer ability to act. Intelligence is energy engaged in solving problems. It is impossible to imagine a human being without energy. And, of course, a leader without energy, physical and mental, simply doesn't exist. Energy is absolutely essential to leadership.

Tension is stored-up energy. To illustrate the absolute essential essence of tension is seen in a human muscle. When your arm hangs relaxed the muscle is not accomplishing its purpose, but when the muscle is tensed preparatory to expression, such as your arm holding a golf club at the point of the back swing, this is an illustration of potential energy. It is tensed and ready to act. When the arms move forward toward the ball and strike the ball with the club, this is an illustration of kinetic energy. The energy is in motion. It is being used.

The following paragraph is based on an article by D. W. Ewing in *The Harvard Business Review*: "Many popular writers and speakers relate tension to unhappiness and lowered productivity, a drain on one's health and vigor. It ain't necessarily so. In fact, tension is the natural way to respond to conflict and to profit from the experience. Conflicts, in turn, are a pre-requisite to progress. Tension inspires people to learn, to improve, to compromise. Enthusiasm is the by product of tensions which arise out of conflict. The zealous thrive on opposition. Tension stimulates the imagination; ideas are born most often where problems exist or where conflicts exist and cry for a solution. The very process of adapting to change is a source of tension. Yet the open mind, the critical mind, the imaginative mind, is also a mind willing to accept the inevitable burdens of tensions that attend these hall marks of maturity and intelligence."[2]

We Can't Stand the Loss

One of the great problems in America today is the tragic loss of energy among people who simply do not believe they have the ability to achieve or do not know how to achieve. These hidden and unused potentialities of people represent our greatest strength and natural resource as a nation. This means, of course, that our engines of potentiality are operating on one cylinder instead of eight cylinders.

Tensions are nothing more than the sensations and feelings all human beings experience when they react to a threat.

Stevenson and Milt in their book, *Master Your Tensions and Enjoy Living Again,* say "We can state that the cause of tension is threat, either physical or psychological. Applying this to your own life you can be sure that if you are a very tense person, it is because your life is full of threat — threat to your bodily failure or threat to your ego. The more threat the more tension. The less threat the less tension."[3]

For example, Madam Curie worked incessantly for forty years conducting tremendous experiments because of the threat to all of the people in the world of disease. She personally had related herself to the hurt of humanity and developed tremendous energy toward the eradication of disease.

Energetic Excellence

Houdini suffered from the threat of others who either questioned his ability as the world's outstanding magician or others whose attainments threatened the position of his world-wide acceptance. Bogardus in his book, *Leaders and*

[2]September - October, 1964, "Tension Can Be an Asset."
[3](Englewood Cliffs, N. J.: Prentice-Hall, Inc., 1959).

Leadership, quotes from Harold Kellock's biography of Houdini, "His training for his various immersion stunts and for feats such as remaining encased in a sealed casket under water for an hour and a half was peculiarly arduous. For months on end, several times a day, he would practice going under water in his own bathtub, holding a stop watch to test his own endurance, lengthening the period of immersion each day until he could stay under for more than four minutes without grave discomfort — accustoming himself to get along with a minimum of oxygen so that he could feed his lungs sparingly with a few cubit feet of air in a little casket and endure for an almost unbelievable time."[4]

Energy is zeal. Moliere said, "Nothing can be fairer or more noble than the holy fervor of true zeal." And Robertson declared, "This world is given as a prize for the men in earnest; and that which is true of this world is truer still of the world to come." Charles Buxton pointed out, "Experience shows that success is due less to ability than to zeal. The winner is he who gives himself to his work, body and soul." And Williams said, "Zeal is the fire of love, active for duty, burning as it flys."

Dr. F. Hall Young says in his poem:

> Let me die working.
> Still tackling plans unfinished,
> Tasks undone. Clean to its end
> Swift may my race be run,
> No laggard steps, no faltering, no shirking,
> Let me die working.

The reason this poem isn't finished is that Young died exactly as he wished — in the middle of the poem. Energy is the zeal to accomplish, the zeal to achieve, the zeal to excel. Work then is the instrument to accomplish the purpose and zeal is the motivating power.

In his book, *Action Power,* Vernon Howard quotes Dr. William B. Terhune, "Most people have plenty of energy if

[4]Bogardus, *Ibid.*

only they would use it correctly. Eliminate any idea that you are weak or you lack energy. If you believe you lack energy you are simply misguided. It is not the expenditure of energy which fatigues you; it is not using enough energy and not using it constantly. Fatigue does no one harm but is instead the first step toward real strength. Be glad you are tired; perhaps you are getting somewhere at last."[5]

Conviction Can Melt a Mob

Energy is courage. One of the strongest motivating factors for courage is religious conviction. A long list of martyrs and people who have given their lives rather than deny their faith is proof of this point. Furthermore, on many other occasions absolute fearlessness has driven the enemy to desert. Many a person has faced the enemy courageously and driven him to surrender. More than once a leader has faced the enemy and come out victoriously by the power of his courage.

Marie Dressler in her biography, *My Own Story,* says, "One may be old or young at 80. As for me, I have the blood of explorers in me and am out to conquer new worlds. I have no sense of having ended my career, but rather of having begun it. I'm starting out with a smile just as in the days when I left home with that cross between a doghouse and a tool chest. I do not like a fight, but if one comes, I shall give it a hug and a kiss. I'm not afraid, for fear means death, and I know that the reaching out, giving out part of me, the part that likes to make people laugh and cry and be happy, can never die."[6]

Energy is motivated by the incentive of conviction. I've seen men in the midst of combat expose themselves at the very expense of their life because of the intelligent selfishness that they wanted to live in a land that was free or die

---

[5] (Englewood Cliffs, New Jersey: Prentice-Hall, Inc., 1963).
[6] (Boston: Little, Brown, Inc., 1934).

for the cause of freedom — so that their loved ones could be free rather than have to live enslaved under tyranny. This intelligent selfishness is what thrusts a man to struggle toward achievement in order that he may be prosperous, the intelligent selfishness is what thrusts a man to struggle toward standing that he may provide for others the necessities and, yea, the luxuries of life.

One of the motivating incentives is recognition. A child will do anything to secure the recognition of his parents and other adults. A youth, in the athletic events, will discipline himself for months and even years of training to be recognized on the score card or on the public address system. And men measure their success by the opinion of others as to how they do their work.

Energetic Incentive in Industry

James F. Lincoln of Lincoln Electric Company gives us the fourfold formula for incentive action in energy: "(1) Challenge the worker's ability. Urge him to do more than he has done before. Give him something to do that is beyond his present ability and give him a burning desire to accomplish it. Put him into conflict with others of his fellows and challenge him competitively to beat the rest. (2) Assure him that there is no limit to his capacities except those that are self-imposed. Urge him to challenge his abilities and to develop new abilities. (3) Lead him to realize that all advancement in the organization is from within and he has unlimited future advancements. (4) Put the development pressure on the leader and expect him to get the best of his men."[7]

This is what develops incentive.

Hazlitt said, "Indolence is a delightful but distressing state; we must be doing something to be happy. Action is no

---

[7]Lincoln, James F., *Incentive Management* (Cleveland: Lincoln Electric Co., 1951).

less necessary than thought to the instinctive tendencies of the human frame." Therefore, happiness, achievement, a sense of success comes when energy produces achievement through courage. Bulwer says, "You see men of the most delicate frames engaged in active and professional pursuits who really have no time for idleness. Let them become idle, let them take care of themselves, let them think of their health, and they die. The rust rots the steel which use preserves."

Courageous action is the energy needed to achieve. Alfred Tennyson said, "I must lose myself in action lest I wither in despair."

What the Mind Can Achieve

The beginning of energy is imagination. The mind must first see the visual achievement of the purpose before action is initiated. The negative use of imagination will diminish and finally stagnate all energy. Do you remember when Don Newcombe, the Brooklyn and Los Angeles Dodgers pitcher, was afraid to fly in a plane? In fact when Brooklyn moved to Los Angeles he threatened to quit baseball; he did not want to fly. Not only was Newcombe an outstanding pitcher, but the best pinch-hitting pitcher in the majors. He just knew that the plane he boarded would crash.

But Don Newcombe went to see a hypnotist. Under hypnosis he was told that the plane would not crash, that he was actually safer than driving an automobile, and the hypnotist bought two round trip tickets for Newcombe and himself and they both flew from New York to Detroit and back. Don relaxed on the plane, enjoyed the trip and learned to fly without fear. Here negative imagination had eliminated energetic action.

Napoleon Bonaparte wrote, "The human race is governed by its imagination."

Conceive and Achieve

Henry J. Taylor said, "Be workers, for the daily work is the daily bread. But also be dreamers, seers of visions, makers of plans, believers in greater possibilities — more and better things for people. Cling to your imagination — to the power of planning and hoping and believing, the power to defeat dullness and stagnation." Remember, whatever the mind can conceive it can achieve but first you must visualize the purpose — the goal that you have in mind. Then you can begin energetically to pursue it and achieve it.

Marcus Aurelius said, "A man's life is dyed by the color of his imagination." And Albert Einstein declared, "Imagination is more important than knowledge." Franz Hartmann said, "The first power that meets us at the threshold of the soul's domain is the power of imagination." William Blake pointed out that the imagination is "the real and eternal world of which this universe is but a faint shadow." And Harold Rugg said, "Imagination is the instrument of discovery. The poet and the scientist agree. Discovery is conceiving in the imagination, or more succinctly, discovery is imagined conception. Imagination is the universal and indispensable instrument of all levels of living in the human world. Our daily lives are dependent upon it."

Charles Dickens said that "he saw his stories and then wrote them down." And Plato declared, "We become what we contemplate." As you can use the power of imagination, of suggestion, of positive thought to determine in your mind's eye what you want to achieve, then you have established potential energy. Only then can you set in motion real energy.

Frank Hiller, the baseball pitcher, used this technique in developing energy: "I passed a powerful energy producing thought through my mind."

Convictions Energize

A famous statesman who had spoken seven times in one day was asked, "Aren't you tired after this much speaking?" He replied, "No, because absolutely in everything I say in those speeches, I am enthusiastic about my convictions." He was on fire for something. He had convictions. He knew where he was going. Thus he produced energetic action.

Dr. C. W. Fuller says, "Enthusiasm is the fuel which fires the imagination; and enthusiasm rises highest when I make the sky the limit. We should let our imagination run riot — then gradually harness it to an idea which seems worthwhile, working from the general to the specific. In this way creative thinking becomes fascinating and develops a pleasant habit which grows and grows with use."[8]

Samm S. Baker in this same book, suggests ten creative mental elements for the creative person. They are these: "(1) Desire to make things better. (2) Alertness — wide open to everything. (3) Interest in digging below the surface. (4) Curiosity — constant spirit of inquiry. (5) Thoughtfulness leading to thorough understanding. (6) Concentration to penetrate matters in depth. (7) Application of energy and effort. (8) Patience to solve problems in detail. (9) Optimism — combining enthusiasm and self-confidence. (10) Cooperation — working perceptively with others."[9]

How Hate Helps

Another factor in developing energetic action is hate. When Hitler was asked whether he thought the Jew must be destroyed he answered, "No, we should have to invent him. It is essential to have a tangible enemy, not merely an abstract one." One of the factors that has motivated the fantastic energy of the Communist people has been

[8]Baker, Samm, *Your Key to Creative Thinking* (New York: Harper and Row, 1962).
[9]*Op. cit.*

world domination. In his book, *The True Believer*, Eric Hoffer makes this statement, "The theoreticians of the Kremlin hardly waited for the guns of the second World War to cool before they picked the democratic west, and particularly America, as the chosen enemy. It is doubtful whether any gesture of good will or any concessions from our side will reduce the volume and venom of villification against us emanating from the Kremlin."[10]

Hoffer states, "Though hatred is the convenient instrument for mobilizing a community for defense, it does not, in the long run, come cheap. We pay for it by losing all or many of the values we have set out to defend." With this I thoroughly agree. However, there is a way when controlled hatred can be an energizing force. It is the hatred of a mother who finds a rattlesnake in the yard playing just a few feet from her little two-year-old child. She will destroy the snake even at the expense of her own life. There is hatred for that that harms one she loves.

Probably the strongest of all motivating factors is self-preservation. When you can lead a people to mobilize all that they are toward the destruction of a common enemy that is already initiating the war — then there is fantastic energetic action. How I remember so well the energy of the American people aroused to fantastic and fanatical loyalty following the Japanese attack on Pearl Harbor on December 7, 1941.

Believe and Energize

Energy is self-image. Our energy comes from our self-image. Our self-image is from the mind which thinks, hopes, fears, produces happiness, becomes sad, remembers, envisions, invents and imagines.

Our self-image is our own conception of the kind of person we are. This is the totality of all of our past experiences, our

[10] (New York: Harper and Brothers, 1951).

failures, our successes, our joys, our achievements, our disappointments, our accomplishments, and the way other people respond to us, especially the way people responded to us in early childhood. This makes up the picture of ourselves which must be a true expression of what we really are.

We must see ourselves as walking across a huge motion picture screen. A vibrant, enthusiastic, achieving individual, we see ourselves head back, shoulders erect, chest protruding, walking forcefully with dynamic purpose, with burning desire and enthusiastic action. We are concentrating upon accomplishing the one main purpose of our lives. So we will give ourselves a daily pep talk convincing ourselves that we are the individual we see pictured before us. This gives us a mental blueprint of what we actually want to accomplish.

Of course, our self-image can be changed, can be adapted, can be improved upon. This is done by relying upon the power of the subconscious mind which consistently produces the commands of the conscious mind.

We accomplish this self-image through the power of suggestion. We regularly and faithfully feed our subconscious mind through positive thoughts, through the association with dynamic, achieving individuals, through the reading of inspirational material, through the playing of inspirational records, by the creating of practical fancies, of dreaming big dreams.

We all have experienced the negative suggestion of a group of people telling one person that he looks bad. If enough people continue to do this the individual will go home sick before the day is over.

Now you can do the opposite through the many means of creating the right self-image. Suggest to yourself over and over in many ways every day that you are achieving the image of the person you want to be.

The Drama of Your Life

This means that you must be the writer, the director, the actor and the producer of your own dramatic life. You must see your goal ahead of you as clearly as if you had already realized it. Bring your goal to fruition through the power of the five senses. For example, establish as your goal the becoming of president of your corporation. You feel the sense of pride that is yours upon arriving at the office on the big day and seeing your name placed as president on the office. You see yourself at the board meeting as the chairman of the board calls you forward. As he congratulates you, you hear the words of congratulation of all the board members as well. You hear the words of inquiry of the press as they ask you questions upon your plans for the future of the company. You taste the many exotic foods that are assured you as a result of your achievements and accomplishments as president of the firm. You now have unlimited travel and can go anywhere in the world representing your company.

Remember, act as if you had already achieved and it inevitably will be yours. James Russell Lowell said, "Greatly begin; though thou hath time but for a line, be that sublime — not failure, but low aim is crime." And Arthur Guiterman said, "God, give me heroes to climb, and strength for climbing."

It was Alexander Graham Bell who stated, "Don't keep forever on the public road, going only where others have gone. Leave the beaten path occasionally and drive into the woods. You will be certain to find something you have never seen before. Follow it up. One discovery will lead to another, and before you know it, you will have something worth thinking about. All really big discoveries are the result of thought."

How Mind Affects Energy

Our physical lives will become what our mental responses

truly are. How important it is that we know in our mind's eye what we want to accomplish. What are the requirements for such action as this? They are the following: Exceptional intelligence; strong, forceful character; and imaginative, original mental response. We must act with the forcefulness of the will, with an unswerving conviction that we are in possession of the only truth in this world. Ours and ours alone is the answer. We must have unquestioned faith in the future. We must actually hate the activities, the things, and the individuals that will limit us from accomplishing our definite purpose. In a sense, we must have no use for the present but a firm conviction that the future holds unlimited opportunity. We must have bold conviction that we do have the loyalty and the cooperation of our associates toward the achievement of our burning desire.

Sun Yat-sen had this self-image. Hoffer in *The True Believer*, quotes: "Sun Yat-sen attracted to himself an extraordinary number of able and devoted followers, firing their imaginations with his visions of the new China and compelling loyalty and self-sacrifice."[11]

Joan of Arc heard visions and led a fanatically loyal people to national victory. Julius Caesar stood at the Rubicon and evaluated the outcome. Because of his hatred of his opponents, because of the forcefulness of his personal conviction, the faith in his cause, and assurance of the loyalty of his associates he was able to say, "The die is cast."

His Conviction Kept Men Free

Historians are now saying that Winston Churchill will go down in history as the greatest leader of the British people. At no time was England in greater danger than 1940. Although he had been out of office for most of his public years Winston Churchill had a forceful conviction that the way of life of the English people was the way of

---
[11]Hoffer, *Ibid.*

life worth preserving, worth dying for. Catch the conviction in these words uttered at Free Trade Hall, Manchester, on January 27, 1940: "Come then; Let us to the task, to the battle, to the cause — each to our part, each to our station. Fill the armies, rule the world, pour out the munitions, strangle the U-boats, sweep the mines, plow the land, build the ships, guard the streets, succor the wounded, uplift the downcast and honor the brave. Let us go forward together to all parts of the empire, in all parts of the island. There is not a week, not a day, nor an hour to lose." And then those climatic words on June 4, 1940, before Commons, "Even though large tracts of Europe and many old and famous states have fallen or may fall into the grip of the Gestapo and all the odious apparatus of Nazi rule, we shall not flag or fail. We shall go on to the end, we shall fight in France, we shall fight on the seas and oceans, we shall fight with glowing confidence and glowing strength in the air, we shall defend our island, whatever the cost may be, we shall fight on the beaches, we shall fight on the landing grounds, we shall fight on the fields, and in the streets, we shall fight in the hills; we shall never surrender, and even if, which I do not anymore believe, this island or large part of it were subjugated and starving, then our empire beyond the seas, armed and guarded by the British Fleet, would carry on the struggle, until, in God's own time, the New World, with all its power and might, steps forth to the rescue and liberation of the Old." Again on May 7, 1941, before Commons he said, "I ask you to witness, that this speaker, that I have never promised anything or offered anything but blood, toil, tears, toil and sweat, to which I will now add our fair share of mistakes, shortcomings and disappointments, and also that this may go on for a very long time, at the end of which I firmly believe — though it is not a promise or a guarantee, only a profession of faith — that there will be complete, absolute and final victory."[12]

This sense of self-image carried Churchill all the way to his death. He even wrote out and prepared his funeral, knowing that the British people would give him the greatest funeral ever to be given a commoner and it equaled anything ever given royalty.

Some Call It Ego

Loud have been the criticisms of General Douglas MacArthur but they came primarily from jealous men. I will never forget those days of doubt in the war of the Pacific when the clarion call to unquestioned and uncompromising victory thundered with conviction from General MacArthur. Upon visiting the Philippines after the war I found that his promise, "I will return," was the clarion cry of the Philippine people who fought the oppressor and his tyranny with such fanatic loyalty — loyalty to liberty and the cause of freedom that causes all men everywhere to stand and marvel. General MacArthur had unlimited energy because of his self-image. In Korea he accomplished the militarily impossible, at least to the Communists, when he landed at Inchon and had his marine divisions ashore before the Communists knew where he was.

One of the motivating principles of life is the compensation that comes in seeking to overcome a physical handicap or some problem of life. Napoleon ruled the world because he was short of stature and had to prove by the brilliance of his mind and his leadership capacity that he stood taller than men physically his superior.

In an article from *Nation's Business Magazine* the question is raised: Which is the best motivator, fear or reward? The answer is, Neither. Experts say that the most effective

[12]Churchill, Winston, *The Eloquence of Winston Churchill* (New York: Signett, 1957).

motivator is a positive self-starting attitude. It is best because it raises the efficiency of both the boss and those who work for him. "Research proves that a self-motivating attitude can multiply a man's productivity," says Paul J. Meyer, President, Success Motivation Institute. He recommends five steps for executives interested in better motivating themselves and their employees: (1) Pinpoint each specific work goal, and dedicate yourself unswervingly toward its achievement. (2) Make a plan to reach your goal. Then stick to an hourly, daily and monthly time table. (3) Keep the payoff constantly in mind. This will make you and your workers success conscious. (4) Don't let thoughts of defeat slow you down. Your attitude should be one of "can't lose" although you should be realistic about your strong and weak points. (5) Develop a fierce satisfaction and pride in your ability to surmount difficulties. Determination to achieve your goals will make you welcome rather than fear road blocks. It will replace doubts with confidence.

How to Live to Be 100

Dr. Flanders Dunbar gives us a recipe for long life: "(1) Good health habits. (2) Marriage. 98% of the 80-year-old doctors are married. (3) Large families. (4) Ingenuity in avoiding frustration. (5) Not worried about getting to the top. (6) Sociability and sense of humor. (7) Not worrying about things beyond control. (8) Ability to sleep soundly. (9) Ability to make a fresh start. (10) No fear of death. (11) Religious conviction."

We get our energy from high purpose. If we have purpose we realize that work is the tool, the instrument, the means of achieving this high purpose. Therefore we look upon work as the necessary and even joyous means of accomplishing that which is worth giving our lives for. Our motto should be: "We have no use for little plans. They have no magic to stir men's blood and they themselves will never be realized." The individual who doesn't like work has told himself that he doesn't want to accomplish anything. He has started to put into action his negative thoughts that will ultimately lead to an emotionally induced illness and chronic emotional fatigue. Not only does he upset himself but he upsets everyone around him. His main problem is a lack of burning desire, a lack of dynamic purpose, a lack of ambition.

Furthermore, we should look upon work as a marvelous therapy, a means of working out our conflicts and tensions, a means of overcoming inner frustrations and conflicts. If you do not like your work it is probably because you do not have a clear-cut picture, a goal, a purpose in life. Certainly I hope you are not working for money. The man who is working simply for money is living from day to day, but the man who works because it is the means toward the glorious end of his dynamic purpose is the man who is on his way to achieve great things. Furthermore, the day goes quicker and passes more joyfully to the one who is using this position and this day as a steppingstone to greater things.

Remember, that will is king. Our emotions and/or intellect are used to express, to motivate, to challenge and to guide the will, the volitional expression.

Epictetus said, "Freedom and slavery — the one is the name of virtue and the other of vice, and both are acts of the will." The French philosopher, La Rochefoucauld, said, "Nothing is impossible. There are ways which lead to everything, and if we have sufficient will we should always have sufficient means." Disraeli declared, "Destiny bears us to our lot and destiny is perhaps our own will." Bakersfield pointed out, "If we cannot shape our destiny there is no such thing." Seabury says in his book, *The Art of Living Without Tension*, "The will obeys the thought patterns or mental images in your mind and operates as they command."[13]

George Elliot declared, "We are all of us imaginative in some form or other, for images are the brood of desire." And Sallust said, "Every man is the architect of his own fortune." Samuel Johnson stated, "Many things difficult to design prove easy to perform." Never forget, your life is what your thoughts make it. It is all up to you. You can have unlimited energy provided you have burning desire, dynamic ambition and high purpose.

Burning Desire Produces Energy

The man of ambition has unlimited energy. Have you noticed how many of the major corporations of America are headed today by young business men? One man started with a nickel and by the time he was forty years of age he was worth five million dollars. Now he is worth roughly 100 million dollars. Certainly, there is more in his life than just making money, but the question is, "How many men can make and keep money who do not provide greater service?" Andrew Carnegie said, "No man becomes rich unless he enriches others."

I have a friend who is the last living man to witness the first successful motor-powered flight at Kitty Hawk, North Carolina on December 17, 1903. What tremendous ambition it took for the Wright brothers to overcome the obstacles, the objections, the criticisms, and the cynicisms of the entire world to achieve their first flight. Of course, their plane only went 852 feet — but ambition was rewarded. Then on Tuesday, February 20, 1962, Marine Lt. Colonel John Glenn was sent into orbit around the earth. This man traveled at the speed of 17,540 miles per hour. He traveled 75,000 miles in the three orbits around the world. Ambition drove Glenn and all his associates in the space program to

[13] (New York, Harper, 1958).

assault that which we did not know about and to make space our servant rather than our master.

Gladstone said, "Man himself is the crowning wonder of creation; the study of his nature the noblest study the world affords."

It is tremendously important that we begin at an early age to place ambition in the hearts of our children. How thrilled I am that my four children all love to read. This is the most important step in their education. Dr. Glenn Doman and Dr. Carl Delacato of the Institutes of Achievement of Human Potential lists the facts about children learning to read before they go to school: "(1) Two and three-year-olds have an unquenchable thirst for knowledge. It is a joyous game for them to learn to read. (2) It is infinitely easier to teach a child to read at the age of two and three than it will ever be again. These children absorb more information than the older children and, of course, the better a youngster reads the more intelligent he will be considered. (3) Small children are being taught to read in many places in the country today. Several hundred two- and three-year-olds with brain injuries are being taught in Philadelphia to read. (4) Tiny children can be taught to read if for no other reason that it makes them happy. (5) In all cases on record in which an attempt was made to teach a small child to read, regardless of method, the attempt succeeded."[14]

Therefore begin at an early age and teach your children to read to instill ambition that they may be energetic. You see, reading failure is closely related to the problem of school dropouts. I'm amazed at the number of adults who cannot read. Do you realize that a child by the age of five has a vocabulary of from ten to twenty-five thousand words? Let's arouse and stimulate this inquisitive nature of pre-school children by challenging them to read and lift their ambition to new heights.

[14]*Our Changing World*, No. 708.

Free Men Are More Energetic

Here in America we are privileged of all people on earth in that the framework of our nation is based upon the fact that all laws are made for the right of the individual. This assures us that every man can achieve if he will but pay the price. John W. Gardner in his book, *Excellence,* says, "No feature of our own society is more highly treasured today than the opportunity for every man to realize the promise that is in him, and to achieve status in terms of his own performance."[15] Woodrow Wilson said that "democracy releases the energy of every human being."

Earl Nightingale quotes the French philosopher, de Tocqueville, who in 1935 wrote, "No sooner do you set foot on American ground than you are stunned by a kind of tumult. Everything is in motion." Zonell said, "Feverish activity seems to obsess these inhabitants of North America." And Alistair Cooke said in 1952, "America may end in spontaneous combustion, but never in apathy, inertia, or uninventiveness."

In Europe all government through all the ages has been kept in control of the hierarchy or the ruling class, not the representatives of the people. There has never been government of the people, by the people, for the people. That is the reason human ingenuity has never been challenged in the old country as it has here in America. Therefore, our very process of unlimited achievement develops amazing ambition because the government is based on the right of the individual and he is a free man.

In 1962 a family from Naples, Florida, left the United States to go to Australia because they said Socialism had so overcome America that there was no opportunity for riches, no opportunity even to make an adequate living. In 1964 oil was struck within one mile of the home this family

15*Our Changing World,* No. 1221.

formerly owned in Naples, Florida. Ambition is a matter of attitude. It is all up to you.

How ambitious are you? What are your opportunities where you are? It could be that you are the main problem. It could be that there are such circumstances that limit you. If you are not challenged, if you are not vitally alert, if you do not see unlimited opportunities ahead, then quit and find yourself other work that will challenge the best of your ability.

Passing the Buck

One of the escape mechanisms that the individual without ambition uses to explain away his failure is, "Let George do it." This statement was coined nearly 500 years ago by King Louis XII of France. His Prime Minister, named George D'Amdoise, was an able administrator and any time the King didn't want to do anything he would let George do it. The person without ambition will assign his own individual responsibility to someone else. Delegation of responsibility to subordinates is a different thing, but the unambitious individual will shirk every meaningful responsibility.

Plato said, "The punishment of wise men who refuse to take part in the affairs of government is to live under the government of unwise men." And James Madison, our fourth president declared, "We have staked the whole future of America not on the power of government, but on the capacity of mankind for self-government." Therefore, take the bull by the horns. Do not shirk your responsibility. Discipline yourself, realizing that your ambition will be cultivated directly proportionate to the aggressive manner with which you take opportunities of achievement and opportunities of service. Lincoln said, "It is your business to rise up and preserve the union and liberty for yourself, and not for me. I appeal to you again to constantly bear in mind that not with politicians, not with presidents, not with office seekers, but with you, is the question: Shall the union and shall the liberties of this country be preserved to the last generation?" And General Carlos T. Romulo, former President of the Philippines and Philippine Ambassador to the United States and United Nations once said, "Take sides; freedom is precious — defend it; it is not cheap, not easy, nor neutral. It is dear, and hard, and real. Take sides for freedom, or you will lose it." You will develop unlimited energy as you accept responsibility. This makes you an ambitious person.

Life's Driving Force

What is the driving force that makes a person ambitious? William Feather said, "Insecurity is the chief compulsive power in the world." And Mark Twain declared, "Hunger is the handmaid of genius." The greatest security an individual can have is a sense of insecurity that drives him to achieve. Dr. Sorokin of Harvard says that we are living today "in our sensate society" — that is, in a nation that has so much wealth, particularly as it is given to its youth until they have been raised with an attitude of the world owes me everything. All the world owes young people is an education and an opportunity in a free society. Clarence Randall, American business executive and author, said, "The young man who reaches his big decision, and chooses business as a career solely on the basis of money, will live to regret it. When at long last he comes to the end of that career he will have nothing but money to show for it, and will have missed the deep satisfaction that will have come to those of his classmates who made their decisions on the basis of how they might render the greatest service to the society that gave them their opportunity."[16] Therefore, the person who wants to develop energy will do so by estab-

[16]*Our Changing World*, No. 1232.

lishing a burning desire, a dynamic life-long purpose with the question: "What can I do to make this free world a better world for following generations?"

How many times have you met an enthusiastic, attractive, well-mannered, poised young man who seemingly had everything but wound up a derelict, a failure? This individual has lacked one thing — ambition. He didn't know where he was going and he didn't know how to get there. The ship that leaves port without a destination winds up a shipwreck. But no captain of any responsible position would leave port without a clearly defined harbor and a definite understanding of how to arrive there. So is it absolutely necessary that the individual know his goal in life and then organize the crew to obtain his goal, establish a responsible ship to take him there and fill the ship with the necessary fuel and supplies to achieve his destination. It will also help you in your achievement if you are in a race. The spirit of competition challenges the individual to excel, provided he has the emotional capacity to rise to the heights of enthusiastic action that competition develops.

There is one other thing very important in developing ambition. You must realize that there had been more scientific discoveries in the last ten years than in all previous historical records of man combined. The largest industry in America is the knowledge industry. Forty per cent of our gross national productivity is the result of it. Twenty-five million people are involved in the knowledge industry. We lose ten per cent of the knowledge we have every year with changing scientific advancement. We add ten per cent of new knowledge every year. Therefore, just to keep up you must improve your knowledge of your vocation at least twenty per cent every year. Actually you need to improve thirty per cent if you are to get ahead.

Yes, ambition is the key to success. You will have unlimited ambition as you develop your life-long goal. You can make a habit of sueceeding.

Excitement and Energy

To develop energy we must be enthusiastic. And enthusiasm comes from two Greek words which means "God in us." When you are dedicated to a cause greater than yourself you will find amazing energy toward the achievement of it. Let your motto be, "We have no use for little plans. They have no magic to stir men's blood and they themselves will never be realized." And "The greatest use of life is to so live your life that the use of your life will outlive your life." Recently Amos Alonzo Stagg passed away at the age of 102. He was forced to retire at the University of Chicago with their compulsive retirement rule. He then took a coaching job at the College of the Pacific. Then when time to retire came there he and his son went to a college in Pennsylvania as co-coaches. And he was coaching Stockton College when he was nearly 100 years of age! What drove this dynamic All-American? He believed in youth and their physical and moral fitness, and he believed that athletics was a means toward achieving physical and moral fitness. His life vibrated with enthusiasm. He had unlimited energy.

Recently I flew from Boston to Miami and was very much impressed by the enthusiasm of the airline stewardesses. These were even more enthusiastic than most and they generally are an outstanding group of gracious, cultured ladies. Between their many responsibilities one of the stewardesses sat across the aisle from me and I asked her how to explain her enthusiastic action. Her reply was, "I love to travel. I love to meet people. I love to see different places and because I love people I consider it a privilege to serve people while they are aboard our plane." Then with a twinkle in her eye she added, "And, furthermore, don't you know that this is the best place in the world to find a husband?" She went on to report that while the national average of marriages ending in divorce is one in four, a stewardess's is only one out of forty-seven. The average airline stewardess serves only eighteen months before she is married, but in that period of time she comes in contact with 8,000 eligible bachelors.

Bill Borden, Manager of Hostess training for TWA in Kansas City, says, "What we have been doing is to recruit and train brides for the nation's bachelors. By the time a girl has finished her six week's course and has been flying for a year, she is a combination mother, teacher, nurse, comforter, confidant, cook and companion. She knows when to talk, when to listen, when to entertain and be gracious. What more can a man want?"

Millie Alfrond, Director of Training for Stewardesses for American Airlines says, "For one thing, the airline stewardess meets more different kinds of men on her job than girls in any other profession. Once she settles on a husband, she no longer experiences that anxious curiosity about other men."

Upon leaving the plane in Miami I said to the stewardess, "The reason you are so energetic is you have discovered the real law of motivation: (1) You have found the joy in giving greater service. (2) You are wisely selfish enough in that you want to be married, to be vitally concerned about your own best interests. Mature is the person who conscientiously wishes to improve their lot in life."

In one of his programs from, *Our Changing World*, Earl Nightingale discusses the sin in selling. He quotes Newell C. Day, now retired in St. Petersburg, Florida, that the cardinal sin in selling is to be uninteresting. You can always tell when the salesman is trying to get something out of you rather than trying to provide a greater service for you. In counseling this is called *empathy*, in *religion* this is called *compassion,* in psychology it is called *rapport,* in education it is called *understanding.*

Energetic Empathy

An old farmer had called his nephew (who was a minister) to go to the city and to visit with him an adjoining farmer who was dying with cancer. The farmer uncle stated to his minister nephew on the way to the hospital: "I ain't much for Bible reading and prayer myself but I believe in it and I want you to do it. My friend, Jim, is dying." The minister stated, that after reading the Scriptures and praying for his uncle's friend — a friend of more than forty years — his uncle did a far greater thing as he reached down and got his friend, Jim, by the hand and said through a broken voice, tears flowing down his wrinkled cheeks, "It kills me, Jim, to see you lying there like that." Here is a true example of suffering with the individual.

If you can't be interested in the other person and in his problems then there is something wrong with you. You are selfish. You are self-centered and you will never make a good salesman. But the individual who sincerely goes forth to meet the needs of his friends that he calls upon, to provide a better service at a smaller fee, will inevitably write the greater amount of business. But he will do far more — he will make a true and life-long friend and both will have unlimited energy.

The person who is interested in the other person will have unlimited enthusiasm and a great zest for living. He will have emotional excitement — and when you lose emotional excitement and enthusiasm you have died mentally.

How many times have you seen a little child with a new balloon and an older brother or sister walk up behind him and stick a pin in the balloon just to be mischievous? Then, of course, the child whose balloon was ruptured became quite unhappy and the furor resulting upset the entire family.

This is an excellent example of so many people who go around with their negative attitudes, pricking the balloons of other people. If you are a dull, uninteresting, unemotional individual, then go off in your own closet and be miserable alone, but don't go around pricking the balloon of emotionally excitable people. After all, they are going places. They are doing things and just because you are jealous — because you won't pay the price that they have in emotional excitement, in conditioning your emotions, in making your emotions your slaves, in a planned program of study and self-improvement to lead you to be an enthusiastic individual, don't go around killing off everyone else who is enthusiastic.

We get our enthusiastic action, our energy from the things we are interested in. Recently a study with students at Georgia Tech in Atlanta, Georgia, revealed that students who had had no sleep for three or four days kept up a high energy level only as long as their interest was kept alive. A study of the Harvard Fatigue Laboratory concluded that 90% of the cause of fatigue is nothing more than mental boredom. Let me illustrate how this happens. Recently I returned from an out-of-town speaking engagement and went immediately to the doctor. I was running a fever, had a strep throat and felt completely exhausted. However, that night I had a speaking engagement two hundred miles away. I literally forced myself to get in the car to drive the distance to fulfill the engagement. Upon arriving at the banquet hall where 700 people were expected, I had some 15 to 20 minutes' opportunity to talk to the Board of Directors of a seven county Production Credit Association. Many young people and families had, for a period of thirty-one years, been loaned money at prevailing bank rates — money to buy and improve farms, dairies, citrus groves, etc. — people who had educated their children, who had been able to come through the depression with difficulty and now were successful, achieving, radiantly happy people. As I talked to these people, my attitudes changed. I soon became vibrantly enthusiastic. The mental excitement of sharing with these people what they had achieved was invigorating. Furthermore, I had some truths in my address that would help them achieve even more. During the process of the meal, with spirited conversation with the mayor of that city and other important dignitaries, I could hardly wait for the introduction and my opportunity to speak. By the time the address was over I was literally free of fever, I was a wonderfully radiant individual, I had unlimited energy. What is the secret? I received a great joy out of what I was doing because it was helpful to other people involved. That's the power of enthusiasm.

Release Your Energy

All of us have ten times more energy than we ever use. The problem is not how to store it or conserve it; the problem is how to release it and to use it effectively.

Your Success Checkup

1. What is James F. Lincoln's four-fold formula for incentive action?
2. List Samm Baker's ten-point formula for becoming a creative person.
3. What are Paul Meyer's five steps to help executives motivate themselves and their employees?
4. List the eleven steps Dr. Flanders Dunbar gives for living to be a hundred.

8.
HOW TO CREATE ENERGY

Is necessity the mother of invention? Do the truly great things accomplished in this world come from necessity? When we look around us and see the tragic failures, the many problems that people find themselves involved in, we wonder why these individuals have not found the answer by inventing the solution to their necessity.

Some of us believe that relaxation is the mother of invention. It is my personal conviction that our best ideas come to us when we are relaxed, when we are working in the yard, playing with the children, driving down the highway, involved in our favorite recreation, whether it be golfing, fishing, or what have you.

The French philosopher, La Rochefoucauld, said, "Ideas often flash across our minds more complete than we could make them after much labor." Our inspiration then comes at the height of relaxation. Our minds do their most creative work when they are relaxed, after the problem has been stated positively, trusting on our subconscious mind for the achievement of the problem.

Let me urge you to try finding the solution to your problem by trusting your subconscious mind to achieve the answer and then letting up from the pressures of the moment and amazingly you will find the solution will arrive suddenly during a period of relaxation.

How often have I stated a problem positively before going to bed at night and found myself awakened and wrote out the solution on a note pad at my bedside or found the solution the next morning upon awaking. All the time we are sleeping our subconscious mind is creatively at work seeking to find the solution to the matter before us.

We can assume then that relaxation and leisure is truly the mother of invention.

The Sleep Machine

In a recent article in *This Week Magazine,* Dr. Cyril Solomon, an American doctor tells of a Russian discovery called *The Sleep Machine.* This looks like a radio receiving set with dials and gauges. There is a mask-like apparatus that covers the face and is about the size and weight of a portable typewriter. This machine produces conditions similar to sleep. The muscles and respiration slow down, blood pressure drops, abdominal breathing takes over from lung breathing. Some have found that even one hour's treatment apparently leaves the same effect of a full night's rest. Editor Erich Lasher tried the Sleep Machine and he said, "I heard it turned on. I felt a tickling on my eyelids, and my eye teeth began vibrating. Both sensations soon stopped. Next thing I knew I awakened. I thought I had been there ten minutes but actually it was an hour and a quarter. My pulse had dropped from 60 to 52, my blood pressure from 134 over 80 to 112 over 78." How much more the dedicated, dynamic person can get done if he only didn't have to spend so much time in the investment of sleep. Imagine how many hours a sleep machine will save.

Marie Ray in her book, *How Never to be Tired,* urges us to use this technique of relaxation before we actually exhaust our physical resources.

For years I have kept a couch in my office. When I find myself tired and can do so I lie down for five, ten or fifteen minutes between conferences. I especially like to do this immediately after lunch. Through the power of auto-suggestion, self-hypnosis, I can breath three or four times and drift off into deep and untroubled sleep. I find that I can tell myself how long I want to sleep — ten, fifteen minutes or whatever — and wake up at exactly that time. I wake up refreshed with renewed energy. You see, the breaking of tension in the middle of the day is wonderfully helpful to the nerves, to the heart, to the entire body.

For the last six or eight years I have worn a wrist alarm. I use it to awaken myself or to remind myself of appointments. Only rarely in these many years has the wrist alarm actually gone off to awaken me. Only when I'm extremely tired does the alarm go off. I wake up one minute before the alarm goes off and change the alarm. One of the psychology professors at Duke University says, "The only way this can be achieved is for our mind to literally visualize the hands of the clock and it awakens us one minute before it goes off." This is another example of the subconscious mind constantly at work while we are asleep.

The Relief of Relaxation

Vernon Howard in his book, *Action Power — the Miracle Way to a Successful New Life,* has a chapter entitled, *Relax Your Nerves and Have More Energy.* Let me quote some of the reasons he gives for effective relaxation:

1. Relaxation speeds your success. You can accomplish far more in a relaxed frame of mind than working under the neurotic power of tension.

2. Relaxation brightens your personality. How often do

we say things — unkind, critical, and condemnatory — when we are tired that we wouldn't dare say when we are refreshed. We are truly ourselves when we are relaxed. We are not ourselves, we are actually out of our minds when we are tired and tense.

3. Relaxation supplies this surprising reward, that is, the reward of alertness. A relaxed mind is a wide-awake mind, and if our minds are alert they can accomplish so much more than if they are tired.

4. Relaxation conquers fear. We have the courage to perform aggressive action when we are relaxed, but when we are overly tense, we perform halted, abrupt and unkind, as well as ineffective action.

Your Energy Generator

You see, tension is literally stored-up energy. Now if this energy is controlled like the water stored behind the dam and released and channeled in productivity and effectiveness, then it is used as it should be. We need the power of controlled tension. But when the water overflows the dam, or becomes so strong it breaks the dam, then disaster occurs.

Dr. William B. Terhune said, "Most people have plenty of energy, if only they would use it correctly — eliminate any idea that you are weak or that you lack energy. If you believe you lack energy you are simply misguided. It is not the expenditure of energy which fatigues you; it is not using enough energy and not using it constantly. Fatigue does no one harm but is, instead, the first step toward real strength. Be glad you are tired; perhaps you are getting somewhere at last."[1]

Do you remember the story of the school teacher struggling to help the little boy put on his boots? After several minutes of strain and struggle they finally got them on. Then the boy said, "It is hard to get them on because they

[1]Edwards, *Ibid.*

are not my boots." The teacher struggled wearily to take the boots off. Then the boy remarked, "The boots belong to my brother, but I wear them because mine are in the shoe shop." The exasperated teacher failed to get to the truth in the first place and this is where we waste so much energy. We move too hastily before we get all the facts. Wise is the person who understands where he is going, determines what his objective is, gathers all the facts and information, and then acts. This is the result of relaxation. If we learn how to relax and get proper sleep and proper rest breaks during the day, then we will be far better prepared mentally to cope with the problems that assert themselves day by day.

It isn't the quantity of sleep nearly as much as the quality of sleep that is important. Immanuel Kant convinced the world that we ought to get eight hours of sleep a night. Now he needed eight hours, but it doesn't mean that the rest of the world needs eight hours. There are people who need at least eight hours sleep a night but for many people — six or five hours may be enough.

How Sleep Heals

Sleep is an individual matter and we should find out how much we need and apply that principle to our life. Just imagine how much more effective the person with five hours sleep a night is over against the eight hour a night individual, for the five hour a night person has 1,095 more hours per year for achievement.

Sleep is a matter of habit and we should determine what is best for ourselves and establish our own routine.

There is a movement in medical science in America today to use the dynamics of sleep to overcome and prevent emotional ills. They actually heal by sleep. They sleep from fourteen to twenty hours a day or from three to twenty days in a row. Russian physicians have extended therapeutic sleep for as long as six months. Professor Pavlov, the Russian scientist, has made amazing discoveries in the power of sleep.

How many of you have stayed in a motel that has a vibrating machine attached to the bed? You place a quarter in the machine and get fifteen minutes of vibration. Reminds me of the story of a couple in California who went into a motel, checked in, lay down for a moment, put a quarter in the machine and immediately the lights went out. There was a power failure. They went out to dinner, came back and retired — still without lights. Sometime in the early morning the light came on and the vibrating machine started its work. Not being used to the vibrating machine the husband jumped up yelling, "Earthquake, earthquake!"

My vibrating chair is an excellent means of helping me relax and the vibrating unit in the bed is a lulling effective means of drowning out the tensions of the day and inducing sleep.

Every person develops in the course of his life certain stimuli that lead him to go to sleep. To some it is a certain position in bed; to others it is a piece of candy; to others it is reading, prayer or any number of other habits that we use to induce sleep. For me it is reading. I keep several books or magazines by my bedside and I read before going to sleep. On occasion, when I am staying at some place where there is not a convenient light for reading in bed I actually have difficulty going to sleep. Actually, restful sleep brings about a complete reorientation in the autonomic nervous system, the midbrain and the cerebral cortex. Our serenity and peace and calmness should be restored through meaningful sleep.

Since approximately one-third of our lives will be spent in sleep, that's nearly twenty-two years, we must learn how to use the sleep effectively. The insomniac not only is frustrated from fighting for sleep, but also from the loss of sleep. His next day's work may be curtailed or even so drastically limited that it would have been better for him to have stayed in bed. Sleep is actually a kind of hibernation brought on by complete muscular relaxation.

The Sleep Soldiers

Marguerite Clark in her book, *Why So Tired?*, quotes a study in Washington by Captain Harold L. Williams, Chief of Clinical and Social Psychology for the Army Institute of Research at Walter Reed, concerning a group of soldiers who were led to sleep for 90 to 100 hours at a stretch. These healthy young men began to see things, to laugh and talk crazily and to show signs of poor concentration.

In one of Williams' tests twenty-five controlled soldiers slept normally in one ward from 11:00 P.M. to 6:00 A.M. while in another ward twenty-five soldiers of the same age were kept awake around the clock for four days. During the day both the controlled and the awake subjects took physical and mental tests, played ping pong or cards, made model airplanes, chanted or listened to records. For the first forty-eight hours both groups performed equally well. Then the sleep-deprived soldiers began to lag. When they showed signs of falling asleep, nurses and corpsmen gently shook them awake. Fatigue came in waves, Captain Williams noted. The men seemed most tired between 1:00 A.M. and 6:00 A.M. Then for a few hours they got a fresh burst of energy.

The most striking changes came in tests requiring mental concentration, such as visual experience or experiments in which a band of letters was passed before their eyes and they were asked to press a buzzer each time an "S" appeared. Half the time the tired soldiers made errors. Next their immediate memory began to fail.

As the soldiers grew more fatigued their senses played tricks on them. They complained of double vision, illusions, that the furniture in the room was moving, specks on the floor seemed to dance. One man thought he saw a dog enter the ward. Another heard his mother call him.

At the end of the experiment the men enjoyed eight to ten hours of sleep. Physically they were unharmed. They performed mental tests as efficiently as before the test. Their personalities were unchanged by prolonged fatigue.

Thomas Edison said to Stanley, "There is really no reason why man should go to bed at all." Edison needed only four hours of sleep. So did Napoleon. On the other hand Woodrow Wilson held out for nine hours a night and Calvin Coolidge, ten. Winston Churchill, although he slept only a few hours a night, made up for it with frequent naps. He is quoted: "A man should sleep in the daytime in order to be at his best at night and a long nap between lunch and dinner is just the thing to banish fatigue."

One New York neurologist says, "Sleeping little actually matters little. What does matter is the anxiety it produces. The poor sleeper must be taught to relax and not lie awake worrying about when he will get to sleep or how he will feel or look the next day if he fails to get enough rest." "When you can awaken without the help of an alarm clock and not be drowsy during the day, you have had enough sleep," said Dr. Robert Felix of the National Institute of Mental Health, "but you had better know your limits. If you need eight hours get them, or the sleep deficit will accumulate uncomfortably and perhaps seriously."[2]

Why People Miss Sleep

Dr. Herman M. Jahr of the Nebraska State College of Medicine says that bad sleepers fall into four categories:

1. Those who have trouble falling asleep. They are the stubborn, aggressive people who take sleep too seriously.

[2]*Our Changing World,* No. 1348.

They end by fighting sleep instead of giving in to it.

2. Those who sleep fitfully and complain of broken rest. This may be the overactive pressured business executive who drops off to sleep soon after retiring then wakes up in a couple of hours with a muscle cramp, a feeling of fullness in his chest, or heartburn. He spends the rest of the night tossing and worrying over what his wife and children would do without him.

3. Those who waken too early and rise tired. These, in most cases, are elderly men and women whose activities, professional and personal, have been restricted by their years. During the day they take frequent catnaps because of boredom and fatigue. They retire early and wake up unrefreshed at 5:00 A.M. They complain of poor sleep but actually they are getting more rest than they need.

4. The real insomniac, a combination of all three classes.

It is quite interesting that in a Gallup poll of eight nations, Americans lead the world in fretfulness in sleep. Some 52% of all Americans stated they had trouble sleeping. By comparison — in Norway, Sweden and Denmark — only 25% had trouble sleeping.

Dr. Nathaniel Kleitman lists a few ideas which bother many Americans:

1. Changing positions frequently hinders sound sleep. Dr. Kleitman says this idea is ridiculous. Changing positions several times during the night helps you sleep better.

2. You must pay yourself back for every hour of sleep lost. Not so. If you were to lose 30 to 40 hours, 10 hours of good sleep would restore your full physical and mental health.

3. You must never fall asleep on your left side. It may affect your heart. Dr. Kleitman says, "Pick your favorite position for dropping off. Very likely you will not be in the same pose when you wake in the morning."

4. Coffee always keeps me awake. It is true that caffeine

in some cases over-stimulates and prevents sleep but thousands of people can drink large quantities of coffee at any hour and still sleep like babies. There are those who just think coffee stimulates them and because it is in their mind they fretfully stay awake.[3]

How to Sleep Better

Here are some ideas to help you sleep more effectively:

1. Pace your late evening activity in such a matter that you lessen the intensity, the excitement of your routine the last hour you are awake. Avoid exciting, highly stimulating T.V. programs. Avoid spirited conversation that excites unnecessarily. Avoid the type of reading that stimulates you mentally.

2. Consider a hot bath. There's nothing like fifteen to thirty minutes in a hot tub to drain out all the tension that you had for the day. Some of us are fortunate to have available a sauna bath which is six-tenths of one per cent humidity. Twelve to fifteen minutes at 240 degrees, then a cold shower, then back for another five minutes, then lie down on a vibrating chair or vibrating table, or vibrating bed, and you are ready to sleep wonderfully.

3. A warm glass of milk is a fine stimulus to sleep. The reason some people do not get to sleep well at night is that they actually are hungry, particularly those who are on a diet.

4. Consider a good walk or riding a bicycle. Dr. Paul Dudley White, the Boston heart specialist, has convinced us of the strong therapy of walking. If you take the dog for a walk before you go to bed at night, it probably will do you more good than the dog.

5. Count your blessings. Acknowledge all the wonderful things that you have. Close your day with prayer and

---

[3]Laird, *Ibid.*

meditation and you will find that there really is peace in your world.

How Sleep Creates Energy

When we do our most restful sleep, our subconscious mind performs its most creative work. In his book, *The Knack of Using Your Subconscious Mind,* John K. Williams tells about the effect dreams had in the life of one of America's great women, Susan B. Anthony. Miss Anthony's friend, Elizabeth Cady Stadon, records in her diary this incident: "Miss Anthony had a remarkable dream. The physician ordered her from Philadelphia to Atlantic City for her health. While in the latter place she had a very vivid dream one night. She thought she was being burnt alive in one of the hotels and when she arose in the morning told her niece what she had dreamed. 'We must pack at once and go back to Philadelphia,' she said. This was done and the next day the hotel in which they had been and ten other hotels and miles of boardwalk were destroyed by fire." Not only is it possible that our minds can warn us of future dangers but also our minds can perform through the power of the subconscious amazing solutions to problems that are before us. John K. Williams also quotes the following statement: "Professor Lamberton of the University of Pennsylvania records that after having vainly worked for some days with a geometrical problem, one morning immediately on waking, he saw the solution given on the wall in front of his eyes."[4]

He Studied While He Slept

Williams quotes another illustration of the power of the subconscious mind: "Dr. Elwood Worcestor was one of America's greatest religious psychiatrists. Twenty-five thousand nervous, tense, distraught people received treatment

[4]Williams, John K., *The Knack of Using Your Subconscious Mind,* (Englewood Cliffs, N. J.: Prentice-Hall, Inc., 1952).

and counsel in his clinic in Boston. He was frequently over-worked helping all those people while at the same time carrying on the work of a large church. He tells of going to bed one Friday night with the realization that he had not prepared a sermon for the congregation for the following Sunday. Suffering from severe fatigue he felt unable to attack the job of preparation. That night he dreamed that a former assistant pastor, Dr. Walter Lowrie, came and re-proached him for his failure to prepare. Then and there Dr. Lowrie dictated a sermon to Dr. Worcestor who wrote it down. The next morning when he awakened, he was dis-appointed that he did not have the inspiring sermon that he dreamed about. Rising from the bed he saw some penciled sheets nearby. There was the sermon in his own hand-writing. He had written it down during the night while he slept. He delivered the sermon and the response of his congregation was greater than usual. Later he included the sermon in a volume called, *Religion in Life*. When Dr. Lowrie read the sermon he said that he had never followed that particular line of thought in his life. Lowrie's seeming presence of the night was not a reality — but the sermon was."[5]

The Reverend Henry Ward Beecher, perhaps the out-standing preacher of the last generation, was a busy man and during one period preached every day for eighteen months. His plan was to keep a number of ideas for sermons incubating. Each night before retiring Dr. Beecher would select one of these incubating ideas, think intensely about it and go to sleep. The next morning he would awake with his idea fully developed for a sermon.

Eleven Steps to Sleep

Elmer Wheeler in his book, *How to Tap Your Hidden*

[5]*Op. cit.*

Sources of Energy, gives the following eleven statements on ways to sleep better:

"1. Stretch. Stretch up. Farther. This takes blood from the brain and puts it into the muscles allowing you to sleep.

2. Eat lightly before bed. It also puts blood into the stomach away from the brain.

3. Don't fight the pillow. It burns energy.

4. Don't think of tomorrow. It burns energy.

5. Think about your childhood and its funs and joys.

6. Read a good book . . . get your mind off your worries.

7. Get a radio that shuts itself off after you are asleep and learn to drift into slumber with a song in your thoughts.

8. Don't crawl into bed; flop into it like a prizefighter who hit the canvas all in a lump.

9. Stay up late. Break the habit of sleeping between certain hours.

10. Be a night hawk on and off. It will do your soul good to stay up all night for a change.

11. Get up with the roosters at times and be as gay as they are."[6]

Unlimited Energy

Unlimited energy comes from the mind. Your thoughts set up electrical and chemical reaction inside the body which creates energy. This is the reason that people with drive, with excitement, with goals and purpose are never lacking in energy. And the more intense our purpose is in life the more energetically our thought waves produce action.

One of the most enthusiastic, vibrant men I have ever met is Frank Bettger. Frank ruined his arm while playing third base for the St. Louis Cardinals and went back to the city of Philadelphia to try to learn a new vocation — selling. He was literally afraid of his shadow but Frank Bettger set

---

[6]Wheeler, Elmer, *How to Tap Your Hidden Sources of Energy* (Englewood Cliffs, N. J.: Prentice-Hall, Inc., 1962).

a purpose and a goal for his life and he drove away fear and despair with energetic action. Today, in his mid-seventies, Frank Bettger is a dynamic and enthusiastic man of action. He acts and talks and thinks like a man one-third his age. He does it with mental pictures. He knows in his mind what he wants to accomplish.

Elmer Wheeler in his book, *How to Tap Your Hidden Sources of Energy*, quotes an interview that Aline Mosby had with Jack Benny: "Jack Benny says, 'You don't look older to people who see you all the time. I really feel thirty-nine. I forgot my age long ago just as I forgot my right name when I became Jack Benny. I do the thirty-nine gag so much on my show that I don't picture myself much older.' "[7] And although Jack Benny is well into his sixties he looks thirty-nine because he thinks thirty-nine. Yes, our mental thoughts, our mental pictures determine to a great extent, not only what we accomplish, but literally how we look.

One of the laws of nature is: We become what we think about. The Bible says: "As a man thinketh in his heart, so is he." I've said on many occasions, "Tell me what a man is thinking about and I will tell you where he will be ten years from now." An early indication of what a man will become is where he spends his money. Show me a man's check stubs and I will tell you what he will become. Therefore, it is absolutely essential that we flash upon the screen of our life the right mental picture. The individual who pictures failure; the individual who pictures fear; the individual who pictures depression; the individual who pictures poverty; the individual who pictures loneliness and frustration — that individual is picturing failure. In this world of bounty and plenty and richness and unlimited opportunity, where we have the finest example of personal initiative the world has

[7] *Op. cit.*

ever seen, for a man to think *failure* actually suggests that he is either sick or emotionally unbalanced at the time.

How a Goal Created Energy

Some eight years ago in St. Louis I met an outstanding young man from southeast Missouri. He had come from a small town to learn everything the big city had to teach about selling. He started out with a high school education selling insurance. He had taken all the training in the small town that that nationwide company could offer. Then he went to the city. He took courses by personal study at night, in the universities, personal improvement courses. He took everything he could. He learned everything he could. When he was making about $30,000 a year he willingly took a cut. He didn't make as much temporarily as an Agency Director as he would as a salesman but, because he wanted to learn, he paid the price and took the cut. It meant that his wife and child had to continue to live in, what to them, was inadequate housing facilities. The dream of their lovely new home had to be postponed. This man, over lunch one day, told me that he had a burning desire — he was to be a $75,000 a year vice-president in the home office of the company by the time he was forty-five years of age. At that time he was thirty-three.

Recently I was in St. Louis. I asked about my friend of burning ambition and they told me he was at the home office, had been promoted to a $60,000 a year position and was one step away from being a vice-president and in only a matter of a couple of years he would reach his goal.

How did he attain it? He pictured in his mind the achievement of his goal. He could visualize himself seated in the chair of the vice-president at the home office. He could feel the fine lines of the grained leather in his chair. He could feel the walnut desk. He visualized his name with the title, *Vice President*, under it on the door of the suite of offices. He visualized the paycheck — $75,000 a year plus bonuses, plus special retirement benefits, plus other features. He knew the benefits it would provide his family, his wife with the home she desired, his child with an unlimited educational opportunity. It meant that in case his health broke he could retire at an earlier age and provide adequately for his family with such benefits as he would receive from attaining his goal. You see, he visualized it in his mind and it became his own.

Energetic Motivation

Of course, the key to building mental pictures is to understand more fully what motivates the individual. Let me list some of the great desires of life:

1. *Self-preservation* — the desire to stay alive. Only the aesthetic and the deeply spiritual individuals really have no fear of death. Those who walk with God so that through His promises death has no fear for them are the few individuals who really welcome death for they have promises beyond. The small per cent of individuals who take their own life, of course, are ill. They are sick. They are out of their minds for the strongest of all desires is self-preservation. The vast majority of us will do anything within reason to stay alive. And of course the emotionally mature individual will avoid those excesses that would shorten his life. A man or animal will fight with beyond human strength when he is cornered in order to preserve his life. I have seen men in military combat do things beyond the reason of human power because they were fighting for their very lives.

2. *The desire for acceptance or importance*. This, of course, is pride and prestige. We are told in the Bible to love ourselves. Seventy-five per cent of the young people applying for jobs or enrolling in college sell themselves short of their real ability. They have more ability than they give themselves credit for. We talk about the one or two

per cent of egomaniacs and a great host of other people react in the opposite direction for fear of being an egomaniac. The truth of the matter is the vast majority of our people need a deeper sense of personal assurance and pride and prestige. Value yourself. You are of great value. You are the chosen of all of life. You live in a nation whose laws are for the good of the individual and all governments subsist to serve the needs of the individual. Cultivate this sense of importance. You are important. Of course your and my freedom ends where the other man's liberty begins. This sense of prestige and pride and importance does not violate the principle of service. The person who truly values himself in democratic spirit will want to share with others all that he has attained. He will want, in the spirit of greatness, to lift others up to attainment and achievement.

3. *The desire for our immediate loved ones* — to provide for our parents, our wife and our children. There are amazing bonds of fellowship of belonging, of emotional security involved in the family and the man who lives for his family is a man who is truly great. This desire for his family's best is one of the driving forces of life. This is what sends a man out in the morning excited about his task, for in the achievements directly resulting from his job his family will benefit. Inevitably when our home breaks up it brings emotional conflicts that affect everyone involved and even the man in his business is not able to do his work effectively.

4. *The desire for sex.* This is one of life's most intimate human relationships and is to be reserved for the meaningful experiences of marriage. We are told that this is the one act that when violated brings heartbreak and grief to each individual involved. When performed as rightly intended it is one of the great motivating forces of life.

5. *The desire to achieve* — the desire to be somebody — ambition. This is an important drive in life and should be encouraged on every hand within the framework of self-

discipline, achievement for a goal, for a purpose. Remember, success is the persistent achievement of a worthy, challenging goal.

6. *The desire to make and keep our money.* Sometimes it is greed. It may be ambition. It has expressed itself in the bargain instinct of the woman who will spend ten dollars to save fifty cents at a sale. That's not wisdom, but it is an expression of the bargain desire. When we recognize that money is an expression of ourselves, that we sell ourselves to our employee — our talents, our time, our abilities, our industry and receive for that time invested, money, then we should value it and not throw it away like those who gamble indiscriminately and those who have dissipated their income in unproductive expenditure. We should ask ourselves, "Where is the place I can invest this money for the greatest good now and for the future?" This is an important desire and should be recognized.

Mental Riches Motivate

Now in building mental pictures you must use both intellectual and emotional stimuli to challenge the will so your subconscious mind will lead you to achieve what your conscious mind commands.

Certainly, it is easier to plant wrong pictures than right pictures. Our minds naturally think negatively. Therefore, it is a matter of personal discipline. You must force out of your life the negative pictures; you must visualize only that which is effective, that which is good, that which is best for you. You will have trouble with your negative mental pictures if you have not learned emotional mind power and will power.

Now you must make these mental pictures highly personal. You must bring to bear in your mind little, seemingly insignificant things to others, but things that to you are very meaningful. For example, say you desire a beautiful home, all that you have wanted all of your life is to be epitomized in this home. Then put it on paper. Draw every little detail — every shrub, every plant, every tree that you want in the yard exactly as you desire it. Put it on paper — the floor plan, everything you desire. Then put it up where you can see it with regularity. Let it be your dreamhouse. Far more important than having the visual representation, it will implant itself in time on your mind until it becomes a meaningful obsession that will lead you to watch your every expenditure so that you may be able to have your dreamhouse. See yourself in possession of your home for it literally is yours the moment you dedicate yourself toward the achievement of it. Actually, all those months and years of planning it, may be more meaningful and more enjoyable to you than when you actually move into it. Possess it in your mind and it truly is yours. Every time you drive by a beautiful home compare it with your dreamhouse. When you see an available lot in the area where you want to live, picture your dreamhouse upon it. And when you talk to a contractor, a builder, a plumber or an electrician, ask him probing questions about features you want in your dreamhouse. Every time you meet an architect or a lawyer, ask him important points about it. And when you talk to a real estate salesman or a home owner, ask him about the values of land. Every time you meet a banker or an investment broker, talk to him about the way to finance your dreamhouse. And when you see an attractive house being built, stop by, go in, look it over. All of this helps solidify the picture in your mind.

The Power of Repetition

Furthermore, repeat these pictures over and over and over again. The more you visualize them, the more you depict them, the more they really become yours. It truly will become a magnificent obsession.

You can have unlimited success directly proportionate to your ability to establish a mental picture of your area of achievement. You must see yourself in your mind's eye overcoming every bad habit in order to achieve, through many newly established good habits, your chief purpose in life.

Abraham Lincoln wanted to be a lawyer so badly he walked forty-four miles to borrow a volume of *Blackstone's Commentary*. He walked nine miles every day to attend a crude log cabin school. No effort of body or mind was too great for him to spend in order to achieve his purpose in life. He saw himself securing the knowledge and the experience necessary to accomplish his goal. His subconscious mind was an obedient servant enabling him to achieve his purpose.

Ernest Holmes said, "We can demonstrate at the level of our ability to know there is a law of unfoldment in man, which says he can advance only by going from where he is to the place where he would like to be." And I love that quote from an unknown source that says, "He placed a crown over her head that for the rest of her life she was always trying to grow tall enough to wear." Have you heard the Indian fable about a mouse that was always upset because he was so afraid of cats? A magician took pity on him and turned the mouse into a cat. Soon it became afraid of dogs so the magician turned the cat into a dog. He immediately began to fear tigers so the magician turned him into a tiger. Then it began to fear hunters. Then the magician said, "Be a mouse again. You have only the heart of a mouse, so I cannot help you."

The person with mental pictures is well-adjusted because he has a goal ahead. He has a glory. He has a purpose and he won't let himself get sidetracked chasing rabbits.

How To Be a More Mature Person

In one of Earl Nightingale's recent programs he suggests

a formula for being well-adjusted. Let me quote them for you:

1. The well-adjusted person is able and willing to assume the responsibility appropriate to each age or period of life as he reaches it.

2. He participates with pleasure in the experiences that belong to each successive age level, neither anticipating those of a later period nor holding on to those of an earlier age.

3. Though he may object to a certain role or position in life, as long as he must fill it he willingly accepts the responsibility and the experience that pertain to this role or position.

4. He attacks problems that require solution instead of finding means to evade them.

5. He enjoys attacking and destroying obstacles to his development and happiness, once he has decided that they are real and not imaginary obstacles.

6. He can make important decisions with a minimum of worry, conflict, advice-seeking and other types of running-away behavior.

7. After making a choice, he abides by it, until new and important factors enter the picture.

8. He accepts the authority of reality; he finds the major satisfactions of life in accomplishments and experiences that take place in a real world and not in the realm of daydreams and make believe.

9. His thinking is a blueprint for action, not a device for delaying or escaping it.

10. He draws lessons from his defeats instead of finding excuses for them.

11. He does not magnify his successes or extend their applications from the field in which they originally occurred.

12. He knows how to work when working, and play when playing.

13. He is able to say no to situations that may provide temporary satisfaction but that over a longer period run counter to his best interests.

14. He is able to say yes to situations that are momentarily unpleasant but that will ultimately aid him.

15. He is able to show his anger directly when injured, not to brood or sulk, but to act in defense of his rights, with both indignation and action appropriate in kind and amount to the injury.

16. He is able to show his affection directly and to give evidence of it in acts that are fitting.

17. He can endure pain, especially emotional pain or frustration, whenever it is not in his power to alter the cause.

18. He has his habits and mental attitudes so well organized that he can quickly make essential compromises if necessary.

19. He is able to bring his energies together and concentrate them effectively upon a single goal, once he has determined to achieve that goal.

20. He would not change even if he could the fact that life is an endless struggle.

Pattern yourself according to this formula and you will have amazing adjustment toward the achievement of your chief purpose.

A person without faith in the final realization of his chief purpose in life simply cannot begin to establish mental pictures. Dr. Ernest Holmes said this in relationship to faith: "Here's a power which every person has but which few people use consciously. One man does not possess this power above another, or to a greater degree. Everyone has it since everyone lives and has consciousness. The question is not, 'Do we have the power?' It is merely, 'Are we using it correctly.' "[8]

Do you remember the poem?:

[8]Edwards, *Ibid.*

> One ship drives east and another drives west
> With the selfsame winds that blow.
> 'Tis the set of the sails and not the gales
> Which tells us the way to go.

Goals Energize

Emerson said, "The world belongs to the energetic." And remember, I mentioned earlier that the person who has a goal can develop unlimited energy toward the achievement of it.

Dr. Marguerite Clark in her book, *Why So Tired?*, had these suggestions about goals:

"1. Psychiatrists suggest: write down on paper the things you want most from life. What is your goal for personal happiness, for professional or business success?

2. Then estimate the amount of energy necessary for achieving these goals. Some in fact will need only a small output; others will claim all the energy you have — and maybe a little more than you think you have.

3. If you pick your goals with care, if you try only for those which common sense tells you are within your ability to achieve, if you mobilize your energy, stick to your purpose, and refuse to accept frustration, the results will prove that will power will see you through, where apathetic acceptance of exhaustion has failed."[9]

"Fatigue actually is not as bad as some people think," says Dr. William Freeman, neuro-psychiatrist of Washington, D.C., "it does not change our capacities; it just diminishes them temporarily. If the symptoms of exhaustion are recognized and something is done about them, fatigue can be a fine education. It teaches us how much we can get out of our body machinery, when the signs of overstrain are, and what to do about them. It is up to us to be everlastingly alert."[10]

---

[9]Clark, *Ibid.*
[10]*Our Changing World*, No. 594.

How Energy Defeats Fear

The person that develops intensive excitement, energetic action about his goal must learn how to overcome fear. In his book, *The Amazing Results of Positive Thinking*, Dr. Norman Vincent Peale gives us the following formula: "For I the Lord thy God will hold thy right hand, saying unto thee, Fear not; I will help thee." Isaiah 41:13. And here are some suggestions for overcoming fear:

1. Know what it is you are afraid of. Pinpoint it. Isolate it. Set it off and see it for what it is. Know exactly what you have to deal with.

2. Discover the origins and reasons for being afraid of this or that. If you are not absolutely sure that you know the reason or reasons, then you had better get some expert counseling.

3. Get the fear out in the open. Divest it of all mystery. Get it out where you can really attack it. Often you will be surprised what a puny thing has been frightening you all the time.

4. Cram your mind full of faith thoughts, for fear cannot occupy the mind when it is full of faith. Remember always that faith is stronger than hate. So, the more faith you have, the less fear you will have. It is that simple, though this process requires some hard discipline.

5. Just do your very level best. You can do no more. Then practice until you strongly develop the ability to leave results calmly to the good Lord.

6. Stand up to your fear and challenge it to do its worst. Usually there will be no "worst," for actually most fear is an unreal bluffing of the imagination.

7. The real fears that have substance in fact, you have what it takes to meet them. God will help you to release the necessary mental and spiritual strength. Pray.

8. Affirm always that by the grace of God you are more

than equal to any fearsome situation.

9. Keep uppermost the most powerful thought and fact of all: "I am not alone. God is my friend, my support. He is always with me."

10. Finally, if you would like further help, send for, *Quit Worrying*, a four-page booklet from the *Foundation for Christian Living*.

The Inner-Directed Energists

The key to great men has always been the inner drive, that inner excitement, that inner goal, that challenged them to excel. George E. Bergman in *Forward* tells us the story of the great people of our world. "Cyrus McCormick was considered a failure as an inventor and the laughing stock of his community because so many of his machines failed to work. When he finally made a reaper that worked, it took him ten years to get anyone to buy it.

"Paderewski as a boy ran from the house and hid in a tree if he saw his music teacher coming to give him his lesson, but he became one of the world's outstanding musicians.

"Fannie Hurst sent eighty-seven stories to one magazine before she made a single sale. Wagner's first piano teacher told him he would never amount to anything as a musician.

"Zola, as a hungry young writer of verse, lived in an unheated attic room in Paris. He set traps for birds on the roof, and if fortunate in catching one, cooked it over a candle and ate it.

"Victor Hugo stood up at a shelf to write, numbering his material as he finished it and then throwing it on the floor. He would later pick it up and sort it out before submitting it to his publisher.

"Charles Steinmetz had his own troubles learning the multiplication table while attending school.

"As a boy Daniel Webster was so shy that he would not stand up to recite in school.

"Horace Greeley's handwriting was so poor that the could not read it himself. He relied on his proofreader Jack Robinson.

"Verdi, the great Italian composer, was rejected for want of musical ability when he applied for admittance to a musical conservatory.

"George Bernard Shaw was painfully shy and self-conscious as a young man. He would walk up and down before a friend's house for fifteen minutes or more, gathering enough courage to call."[11]

Yet each of these people became outstandingly successful because they had in their mind's eye a purpose, a mental picture of what they wanted to accomplish and nothing would keep them from the accomplishment of it.

George Westinghouse's teachers thought him dull and backward. He was asked to leave Union College at the age of nineteen, after he told the President, "I would like college very well if I had time to give my mind to my studies." Yet he was only twenty-two when he developed the air brake and organized the company to manufacture it for the railroad industry. And during his lifetime he received patents on 361 inventions, an average of one invention every six weeks for forty-eight years. He founded sixty companies.

Thomas Edison did poorly in school and was educated largely by his mother and by reading at home.

Remember the promises of Job 22:28 to the child of God, "Thou shalt also decree a thing, and it shall be established unto thee: and the light shall shine upon thy ways." Also, the Bible promises, "Whatsoever ye shall ask in prayer, believing, ye shall receive." Again the Bible assures us in Matthew 9:29, "According to your faith be it unto you."

11*Our Changing World*, No. 1347

How Our Emotions Control Energy

Let me explain to you what happens when we create a mental picture. Our mind affects our entire physical body. Dr. Alexis Carel in his book, *Man, the Unknown,* says: "Each state of consciousness probably has a corresponding organic expression. Emotions, as is well known, determine the dilation or contraction of the small arteries, through the vasomotor nerves. They are, therefore, accompanied by changes in the circulation of the blood in tissues and organs. Pleasure causes the skin of the face to flush. Anger and fear turn it white. In certain individuals bad news may bring about a spasm of the coronary artery, anemia of the heart, and sudden death."[12] Now the same principle is at work when you establish in your mind's eye a worthy challenging goal. Once you have dedicated yourself toward this goal a sense of pleasure, of peace, of serenity comes over you. You have peace in your heart because you are giving of yourself to something that is worthwhile, to something that is altruistic, to something that will benefit others, to something that will bless all mankind. Then, secondly, you will feel a sense of excitement, of enthusiasm, renewed energy, unlimited energy because you have a goal that is greater than yourself. Let your motto be: The greatest use of life is to so live your life that the use of your life will outlive your life. Thirdly, you will come in at night tired, exhausted, but you know that what you have done has led you one step closer, one milestone closer to the realization of your goal. Now you are living for a purpose. Now there is joy, a sense of achievement, peace, happiness, serenity, excitement — all of these wonderful, positive emotions working for you. Your life takes on a deeper dimension, another dimension and you find yourself an outstanding, achieving individual.

---

[12](New York: MacFadden, 1961).

A Fabulous Story

What is the difference between one boy and another? How is it that with two boys of equal background, family tradition, education and opportunity, one excels unusually and the other rocks along in mediocrity? Let me tell you the story of two boys both of whom became outstandingly successful in different areas of life. Earl Nightingale tells us this story of a young English boy on a visit to a rural community in Scotland who set out to enjoy a swim in a small lake. He was seized with cramps while some distance from the shore and began calling for help. A young farm boy working in a nearby field heard him, plunged into the lake, towed the drowning swimmer to shore and administered first aid. In a short time the visitor recovered and was able to return to his home in London. The farm boy, forgetting the incident, continued to perform his daily chores on the farm.

Many years went by and the two boys met again. This time the city youth came to the rural community to ask the farm boy who had saved his life what plans he had formulated for the future. When the farm boy frankly confided that his ambition had always been to study medicine, the youth from London revealed that he and his parents were ready, in fact, eager to place at the young farmer's disposal the money he needed for his education.

More years passed. The farm boy attended medical school, graduated with high honors and embarked upon a career of scientific research. Eventually in 1928 he made a discovery that was to save uncounted millions of lives. In his laboratory he found germs could not exist in certain vegetable molds. He discovered penicillin.

The one-time farm boy was now Dr. Alexander Fleming who was to become a Fellow of the Royal Society, who would be knighted by the Queen and win the Nobel Prize for his scientific achievements.

But what about the boy from London whose life Fleming had saved and through whose financial assistance Fleming had been able to study medicine?

Well, that's a rather interesting and essential part of this story.

During World War II that Londoner was stricken with pneumonia while on a journey in the Near East. He had made the trip to meet with Franklin Delano Roosevelt and Premier Stalin for a series of important conferences.

His condition became alarming. Back in England the drug invented by the one-time farm boy was ready to be flown to the sick man's bedside. Within a few hours the miracle drug, penicillin, had performed its mission and it added another illustrious name to the long list of those whose lives had been saved by its amazing properties. For the second time Alexander Fleming had saved the life of Winston Churchill.

It is quite interesting that two different boys from decidedly different backgrounds, both attained such outstanding success in their different fields. But the answer is — they had a mental image of what they wanted to accomplish. Alexander Fleming could imagine himself in a laboratory, investing all of his time, ability and dedicated talents to scientific research. He personally committed himself. Winston Churchill knew that the destiny of world leadership had been placed upon him and he paid the price. He became one of the world's outstanding statesmen. These men knew in their mind's eye what they wanted to accomplish and let nothing keep them from it. The person with a dream, the person with a glory, the person with outstanding purpose, who has learned to focalize this purpose in the mental images of his brain has determined he will stand tall above the crowd.

Cut Flower People

Someone has said that we live today in a "cut flower"

generation. People without roots; people that are soon to die. Well, we do have many such. Probably most people are of the "cut flower" category. But I want to tell you, my friend, you can be a sturdy oak. But an oak didn't become an oak in a few years. We have in South Florida the Australian pine, a very rapid growing tree, imported from Australia. It grows tall and it has a needle similar to the American pine. You can cut it into shrubs or you can let it grow tall into trees, but when the first hurricane or big wind blows it is so brittle that it will break and fall over the road. But look at the oak. It takes decades and centuries to grow a great oak but, my friend, it doesn't topple in the wind and it will stand for centuries to give haven to every weary passerby, to give a harbor to millions of birds over its span of life and finally to be cut down and made into beautiful hardwood floors. So early in life develop a purpose and build burning desire through the mental image in your mind of what you believe God and your will wants you to accomplish. George Eliot has said, "What makes life dreary is the want of motive."

You see, high purpose is like some heavenly pied piper playing an alluring melody that drives from our minds every other sound, enticing, compelling and with rapture, leading us to attain what we have established as a mental image for our achievement. This mental picture is your key to success.

Do you remember those days as a youth when we would imagine amazing things? Something terrible has happened when we've crowded out all imagination in adulthood. When hope dies there is nothing else. Imagination is the perpetual beat of hope, the persistent command of our mental picture, emotionally exciting us to achieve our date with destiny. Furthermore, imagination makes it a game and overcomes the drudgery. Imagination creates curiosity that wants us to look over the next hill, that tells us the grass in greener in the next field and assures us that life does have some interesting and wonderful experiences ahead. You see, what we believe about our responsibilities here determines what we are.

Don't Sit Out Your Life

There was a man in India who was sitting by a river doing nothing. It seemed to be this was his entire purpose in life. An American noticed him for some days and then went up and engaged him in conversation by asking him, "What are you doing here?" And the man replied that he believed in incarnation, that he believed that we had lived other lives before and would live many times afterward so he said, "This life I am sitting out." Now, my friends, I know a lot of people who don't believe in incarnation that are sitting out this life — no purpose, no plan, no goal, no excitement, no joy, nothing but death. When we die upstairs we are simply vegetating. Some people die at thirty and are buried at seventy. I know some people who have been embalmed but haven't been laid away yet.

There is a story written by a Russian author about a young man who was to be executed for murder. As dawn broke he stood at the window of his prison cell where he could see over the prison walls to the countryside beyond. It was summer, and at the first light of the beautiful day a change came over the young man. Suddenly he became tremendously interested in seeing the first faint rays of the sun touch the leaves of the trees. He noticed the beauty of the earth and the green of vegetation and as he gripped his bars and stared out upon the scene which had been played every morning for countless centuries, tears started down his cheeks. He realized that he was seeing the glory, the beauty, the marvel of the world for the first time in his life. It took his death for him to begin to live. Don't be like that.

How Free Enterprise Enables Energy

Of course, for a person to be able to develop excitement, hope, vibrancy and expect unlimited achievement there must be other conditions round about him. The principle of it all is *free enterprise,* a system where man has unlimited opportunity of achievement. Free enterprise first was established in the heart of God when He allowed man to own and to control the earth. Then it was rediscovered in the constitution of these United States where the precious principle of government of the people, by the people, for the people, was found and has been practiced. Here government's purpose has been to assist man, not to control or dominate him. Dr. Ludwig von Mises says, "The reason free enterprise and capitalism has been so outstanding in the United States of America is because there the government started interfering in the affairs of business later than in other countries of the world."[13] Do you realize today that in some of the Socialistic nations which have so many so-called ideal plans such as *socialized medicine* and *social security* and *hospitalization* provided free and these other things, that in these nations you have an almost complete lethargy or letdown in initiative because the hope of individual achievement is stymied? Their society is fixed so a man can't succeed and fixed so a man can't fail.

In Norway, for example, there is a progressive income tax that works like the gallows — the higher you go the harder you fall. For example, everything a person earns over $8,400 a year is taxed at eighty per cent. That's eighty cents for the government; twenty cents for the citizen. In Norway, a visit to the doctor will only cost you fifty cents; the government pays the rest. But is it worth it when eighty per cent of your income above $8,400 goes for taxes? Never forget,

[13]von Mises, Ludwig, *The Anti-Capitalistic Mentality* (Princeton, N. J.: Von Nostrand Co., 1956).

my friend, the greatest expression of personal initiative the world has ever seen is in the United States of America and also remember that in 1848 a paranoid Jew by the name of Karl Marx said that he would destroy capitalism by two principles: the progressive income tax and the destruction of all laws of inheritance.

You see, I am an old-time individualist and idealist who believes that the American dream was patterned upon the principles of God, that men ought to be free and governments ought to assist them to be free and not to control them and dominate them.

If your mental picture is to be effective, you must have the right attitudes. Our attitudes control and manage all of our lesser habits; therefore, we must control our attitudes so we can have complete control over our life.

Value Yourself

Dr. David Harold Fink in his book, *Release from Nervous Tension,* suggests several needs of the human being. They are in three categories:

1. *Physical* — the need for food, clothing, shelter, exercise, relaxation.

2. *Personal* — the need for self-expression, new experiences and amusement.

3. *Social* — the need for security, friendship, status and love.

Wise is the man who will admit these needs and will systematically set out to satisfy these needs; therefore, overcoming the tensions and frustrations that come when these are not met. Our attitudes to a great extent are the result of having satisfactorily met these needs. For example, take the social need Dr. Fink spoke of, the need for security. We are not talking here about economic security alone. We are talking far more about emotional security, the sense of belonging and the sense of contribution to others in helping them along. Everyone needs friends. There is a popular song today: "People who need people are the finest people in the world." In order to have a friend we must be a friend. Lonely hearts don't believe this, but it is true. Getting and keeping and making a friend is the easiest thing in the world. You make friends simply by being friendly. And, furthermore, status is important for this self-appreciation, this is self-confidence and the root of these two expressions lies in our value of ourselves. Remember, you are a precious person. You are important. You must be able to have faith in yourself. You must love yourself. I am not talking here about adoration. I am not talking here about self-worship. That is false and wrong. I'm not talking about an egomaniac. I'm talking about self-respect and self-confidence and worthy evaluation of yourself as an important individual. Now, of course, you need to feel that you are wanted, that you have a contribution to make in life, that you have a purpose to achieve, that you can leave a better world and this leads you to excitement on your burning desires, in your mental pictures.

Another thing a mental picture does for the individual is to enable him to carry a heavier load. How many times have you seen a bridge unsafe for loads exceeding two tons? You had better not take a three-ton load across that bridge. It may fall in on you. How many of us find ourselves at times carrying too much of a load personally? You see the reason is that our mental pictures have not led us to lighten the load. What I mean is this — if you have a dream of your house and you know what you want to accomplish, it is a beautiful house, it has been forming in your mind for years; then every day that you dream of it and can picture it, you are building it a little bit at a time. You are putting another brick in its place. You are adding another bit of shrubbery in the yard. You see, the load isn't heavy. The load is light because it is a part of a lifelong dream. One of the best ways to lighten your load is to see that that day's work is a contribution to the achievement of what you have burning bright in your mind, in your mental picture.

The person who works for no purpose feels that each day's work is a prison house and he is never quite free. But the man who sees each day as a stepping stone to life's greatest achievements in achieving his mental picture, that man is free, wonderfully, amazingly, mentally free. He is climbing above the clouds on the journey of his heavenly vision — his magnificent obsession. You see, every day we are sculpturing our dream. We are molding it, building it, planning it, dreaming it and achieving it. Therefore, you have the joy of creativity. You have the joy of daily investment. You have the joy of hope and imagination. You have the joy of vibrancy and participation and one day you will have the joy of receiving your burning desire.

You Control Your Face

When Abraham Lincoln was assembling his cabinet after his election to the presidency for the first time a certain man was recommended for an official position. Lincoln replied, "I don't like his face." An advisor said, "Mr. President, are you going to reject a man because of his looks? He can't control his looks." President Lincoln said, "After a man is forty his looks reflect his character and personality. He can affect his looks."

Someone has well said, "At sixteen you can't control your looks but at sixty you are responsible." Our facial expressions reflect our mental attitudes and the individual who has strong self-image, practicing mental pictures for years does literally control his countenance. There is an old African proverb which goes, "If your face is ugly, learn to sing."

Some of the most radiant personalities I have ever known are individuals with physical difficulties. They made their problem a steppingstone to success. I remember a dear friend. He and his wife have only one child and this child has physical difficulties. Through the power of their dynamic personalities she has developed dynamic personality, and today she is one of the most radiant individuals I have ever known. You see, her mind, her mental pictures actually changed the situation.

Let me quote again those words from Dr. William James, "The greatest discovery of my generation is that we have learned that we can alter our life by altering our attitudes of mind." You see, we become what we think about and our attitudes either set us free from the slavery of negative emotions or our wrong attitudes put us in a cage and throw away the key.

We are a nation of hero worshipers. What boy doesn't want to play baseball like Mickey Mantle or Joe DiMaggio or Babe Ruth or Stan Musial? One of the tourist attractions of the city of St. Louis is Stan and Biggie's restaurant on Oakland Avenue. Stan is a wise man and very public-relations conscious. He seeks to go by the restaurant and spend some time both at lunch and at dinner as often as he can when he is in town. He will hand out personally autographed pictures and inscribe them to particular individuals. When a man is in town for a business appointment he will often go to Stan's and have Stan address an autographed picture to his son or his daughter.

President Johnson has commented on many occasions of what Franklin Delano Roosevelt and Speaker of the House Sam Rayburn's influence was in his own life. If you don't have a hero you ought to. Let me make a suggestion of how hero worship can help you with your self-image.

How Heroes Help Our Energies

Pick out the outstanding traits from as many achieving individuals as you can. For example, the oratory of Winston

Churchill; the dedication to duty of General Douglas Mac-Arthur, who was overseas from the late thirties to 1951, not even returning to the Continental limits of these United States, he was so dedicated to his duty; the ability to persuade people of President Johnson; the intellectual wit of the late President John F. Kennedy; the wholesome joy by which he plays, with all the conviction of his being, the game of baseball of Willie Mays; the sense of service to others of Herbert Hoover and Bernard Baruch; the compassion to help the hurt of humanity of Dr. Tom Dooley and Dr. Albert Schweitzer.

Now put the composite of these dreams in your mind and try to become the kind of person these individuals have become. Imagine yourself achieving in every area. Read about them. There must be the emotional excitement of daydreaming. Pick out individuals that you know more intimately, people you know personally, citizens of your community, get to know them, ask them for appointment, take them out to lunch or to dinner. You see, great men delight in sharing with others what they have achieved. They want to hand on to succeeding generations the things that they have attained.

Recently I had the privilege of speaking to a large group of salesmen and manufacturer's representatives of Taylor Machine Works of Louisville, Mississippi, meeting at the lovely resort hotel Broadwater Beach at Biloxi, Mississippi. These men and their wives had gathered from all across America and from Canada, representing the several divisions of Taylor Machine Works. After my address on *How to Make a Habit of Succeeding*, when I told about the possibility of outstanding achievement through persistency, enthusiasm, the power of the subconscious mind, etc., one man came up to me and asked, "But don't you ever get tired of working all the time, doing the same thing all the time?" And my answer to him was this, "No, because making a habit of succeeding has within it the formula of enough variety and change that keeps your life vibrant and enthusiastic." Only the totally dedicated individual can consistently stay at one task day in and day out, week in and week out, month in and month out, year in and year out, without becoming tired. And frankly there are so few of us totally dedicated to our task. The vast majority of us need enough variety in our daily and weekly schedule in order that we can return to our main task with enthusiastic action.

Refresh Yourself

Getting away from the pressures of the office to play golf or to play tennis or go fishing or do your favorite hobby, is not a deviation nor a departure from your main purpose but actually is a refreshing experience that will help you better achieve your main purpose. Furthermore, as your conscious mind continues to tell your subconscious mind, through the power of the persistant mental pictures that you are flashing upon the screen of your dreams, then you need time for your subconscious mind to bring to realization the commands of the conscious mind. As the architect of the conscious mind has been sending the plans to the contractor, the contractor must have time to get the materials, and sometimes they have to be secured from some distance, to assemble them on the grounds, to line up his men and then to build the building. If you force him to build it hurriedly he may use inferior materials or inferior building methods that could bring about a break in the structure. Give him time to do an adequate job. I would much rather take a longer period of time and build the building properly than to build it haphazardly and then have trouble in the basic structure.

Now as you get away from your main task for deviational and recreational and creative activity, your subconscious mind will continue to work and often-times through the power of leisure will come up with the answer much quicker than under the pressure of your daily routine. I have found it advisable when I get stale studying over an extended period of time to get up, go out and make a few calls; or I call for a conference; I arrange a staff meeting; or I go do some other phase of my responsibility. But there is enough variety in most everyone's job, if he will plan it effectively that even in the framework of his regular work duty he can remain creative. Just remember that change is a vital, life-giving, energy-producing aspect of life.

The word *relax* means "to divert as the mind." There is a song that says, "Let go and let God." And we need to get away from the pressures of responsibility by relaxing our mind as well as our body. Fatigue is good and necessary in life, but sustained tension on the rubber band will soon break it. The rubber band will expand and perform its work, then when you relax it you will find that the fatigue is removed and it can once again be expanded to perform its responsibilities. This is true in metal. Tension in metal if continued will bring about fatigue and it finally will break.

Psychic Success

In her book, *You Can Change Your Life Through Psychic Power,* Jo Anne Chase gives us the ten-point formula for psychic success. Here they are: 1. Believe. 2. Relax. 3. Tune in. 4. Accept. 5. Know. 6. Act. 7. Practice. 8. Develop. 9. Retain. 10. Expand. I urge you to get this book. You can get it in paperback from Pocket Books, Inc. You can change your life through psychic power. It will help you create the right mental image.

Here's an excellent example of how a dream, a mental image, can come to a practicality and realization. In Elmer Wheeler's book, *How to Sell Yourself to Others,* he tells about Mr. Woolworth of the F. W. Woolworth Company standing in New York talking to an ambitious young architect one day. This was six months before the construction of the famous Woolworth Building. He had no idea at all about constructing a building there. The architect said, "Mr. Woolworth, you see that plot of ground over there? That is where I am going to build you the tallest building in the world." That startled Woolworth and he began day-dreaming, building his castles in Spain, but all the time it started the process in his mind of building the tallest building in the world. Six months later the construction actually began.

Recently a woman wrote Earl Nightingale the following statement: "My biggest problem is not having enough confidence in myself. My husband is a good guy, but in some ways he is inconsiderate. He never praises me and in front of other couples he always seems to run me down and make himself look so much smarter. I love him but it still hurts and I believe that is most of the cause of my not having any confidence in myself." Someone has well said that one of the true ways of determining the size of a man, the bigness of a man, is how he treats his wife and his family. Some men indicate they could write the book, *How to Win Friends and Influence People*, at the office but at home they are tyrants.

Family teasing is one thing, but when it continues to be family argument and running down the other individual, it becomes dangerous to the esteem of the person. One of the finest things people can do in marriage is to build up the self-esteem of the other individual and the other members of the family.

He Built His Bridges

One night at a game a man said to his wife who was his partner, "Darling, I just want to mention while I'm thinking about it that you have more wonderful qualities than any person I've ever known. And I love you very much for every one of them." Of course his wife beamed and everyone in the room smiled at this fine compliment. Then the man paused and said kindly, "But I'm afraid playing this game isn't one of them." Of course this brought the house down. He had built her up high but the statement was made in such a gracious manner that she wasn't hurt and undermined.

You see, we each need our own self-esteem established more and by giving it to others they in turn will give us the compliments we need to help create the right kind of mental pictures and then to sustain them after we have created them.

Let me urge you once again to secure in permanent form the address by Dr. Russell H. Conwell, who lived from 1843 - 1925, *Acres of Diamonds.* This is a true story. It is true because it has happened to hundreds, thousands of people in the same number of situations down through the years. Dr. Conwell, in telling this story literally around the world raised six million dollars to found Temple University. You remember the story but let me tell it again to drive its truth home in our minds. A Persian farmer was told by a visiting friend about diamonds and he sold his farm and traveled the world seeking to discover diamonds. After he had exhausted his health and his financial resources, and was penniless, in poor health and despondent, he threw himself into a river and drowned.

The man who had bought his farm found an unusual looking stone in the creek bed which ran through his farm. He put it on the mantle as a curio. The same visitor who had told the first owner about the diamonds came through and told him it was one of the largest diamonds ever found. It was worth a king's ransom. They dug there on the farm and discovered the world's largest diamond mine—Golconda.

Your Chief Purpose

In establishing in your mind the mental pictures to help you achieve your chief major purpose in life, let me suggest that you consider three things. If you would ask the average person what he wanted, I believe these would be at the top of the list: *health, wealth* and *happiness*. There are few of us who are appreciative of our health until we have lost it or run the risk of losing it, or we have seen someone else who is not healthy. How tragic it is that we live such hectic lives that we fail to be thankful. I well remember those lines:

> To gain his wealth he spent his health,
> And then by might and main;
> He turned around and spent his wealth
> To gain his health again.

The second thing that most people want is *wealth*. Most people think that in the accumulation of things there is all that a person desires. They somehow think that happiness is in the accumulation of things. The person of good health and dynamic purpose and unswerving dedication to the single aim in life can become wealthy, provided he is willing to get along, to live on a good deal less than he earns and have the ability to save and invest the difference. In our world today any person can get rich if that's what he makes up his mind to do and sticks persistently to his plan. Recently I read about a man who had spent his entire working life as a mail room clerk and had amassed a fortune in the millions of dollars. He had started without a penny. We read with some regularity in the papers about some lady who on a school teacher's salary or a clerk's salary or a secretary's salary, by wisely investing in the stock market and other investments, has become amazingly wealthy. But were they happy? That's the next item that we want to mention. Happiness comes not from attaining but more from dedicating ourselves to a cause greater than ourselves.

Do you realize that most children are happier while they are going to school than during the vacations? They wouldn't admit it, but it is so. Most people are happier during the year they are working, anticipating their vacation, than they are actually during their vacation. When we have something worthwhile to do, a cause greater than ourselves, and we are dedicated to that cause — then we really are happy.

One of the exciting books in my library is, *The Magic Power of Self-Image Psychology*, by Dr. Maxwell Maltz. Dr. Maltz develops the idea that what we think of ourselves we become. He tells us that there are six things that we ought to do to throw away our mask and to develop our real personalities. Here they are:

"1. Do not be afraid to be different. Dare to be different.

2. Lose your fear of perfect people. There is no one who is perfect but desire to become more perfect every day of your life.

3. Try to be more spontaneous. Learn to let go. Let yourself loose from the inhibitions that control you.

4. Rely on yourself.

5. Squelch your self-critical thoughts. Give yourself a daily pep talk.

6. Shed your mantle of dignity. Some people are so dignified you have to pinch them to really know if they are alive. Be yourself. Quit forcing yourself into a false mold. Determine the kind of person you want to become and let nothing in this world keep you from attaining that goal."[14]

Dr. Maltz quotes from the book, *MacArthur 1941-1951*, by Willoughby and Chamberlain: "General MacArthur had this belief. From the day of his confident parting message to the Filipinos, *I Shall Return*, no deviation from MacArthur's single-minded plan is discernible. Every battle action in New Guinea, every air raid on Rabaul or PT boat attack on Japanese barges in the Bismarck were a mere preliminary for the re-conquest of the Philippines." And the world gave him praise for the single-mindedness of his purpose. Then when he moved into Japan he set himself unswervingly to

[14] (Englewood Cliffs, New Jersey: Prentice-Hall, Inc., 1964).

the task of making that nation a democracy, and history will prove that one of the greatest feats of statesmanship the world has ever known was accomplished by General MacArthur in the complete change of political life of the Japanese people.

She Became Somebody

Another interesting biographical sketch from Dr. Maltz' book is the story of Althea Gibson, the negro tennis star, in her book entitled, *I Always Wanted to be Somebody*, in which she described her concept of success: "I always wanted to be somebody. I guess that is why I kept running away from home when I was a kid. Even though I took some terrible whippings for it. It's why I took to tennis right away and kept working at it, even though I was the wildest tomboy you ever saw and my strong likings were a mile away from what the tennis people wanted me to do. I was determined that I was going to be somebody too — if it killed me."[15]

Emerson has said, "Self-trust is the first secret of success." Therefore, if you will believe in yourself you will succeed.

Edmund Burke, the outstanding British statesman, said, "Those things which are not practical are not desirable. There is nothing in the world really beneficial that does not lie within the reach of an informed understanding and a well-directed pursuit."

Dr. Maltz suggests a four-point formula on how to achieve success:

"1. Encourage your success mechanism by discarding your negative failure thoughts. Picture yourself as a success. Capture in your mind every happy experience that comes to your subconscious.

2. Set definite, realistic goals for yourself.

3. Understand your rights. Tell yourself that you are a deserving person. Think of yourself as being valuable in the

[15]*Our Changing World*, No. 1319

sight of God and in the sight of others.

4. Believe in yourself. Establish a climate of self-confidence through a regular reading program and an inspirational development program. Believe that you can accomplish anything in this world you set out to accomplish."[16]

There is a price to pay for failure. There is a price to pay for success. The person who pays the price for success is far happier than the person who pays the price for failure.

In Your Own Mirror

Recently it was my privilege to be on the program for the Florida Lumber Dealers Association at the Doral Hotel on Miami Beach. On the back of their breakfast program one morning when Dr. Ken McFarland brought a most interesting and inspiring address I found this quote. I want to pass it on to you. "Throughout history most great civilizations that have declined were victims of stagnation rather than conquest." Apathy, indifference, detachment led to decay. In our own country today we find more people who prefer the role of spectator rather than participant. Whenever a problem arises the spectator asks, "Why don't they do something?" They can't help the police to maintain law and order. You can. They are not responsible for the condition of your schools. You are. They can't give your community good government. You can. Every civic group, every business, every sports club, every worthwhile institution began with a need, a vision, turned into a reality by someone alive, responsible and innovative. To the people who sit back and ask, "Why don't they do something?" we ask, "Why don't you?" Well let me try to explain why you don't. The reason is you do not have a mental picture in your mind of what you ought to attain. You have just been living — should I say breathing, existing — day by day. Directly proportionate to your capacity to develop in your mind's eye a picture

[16]Maltz, *Ibid*.

of where you ought to be at the height of your years of attainment will you succeed or fail. It is all up to your mind and your mind's eye.

One of the truly amazing individuals in this world today is Mr. Paul J. Meyer, President of Success Motivation Institute of Waco, Texas. Here are two quotes I would like to pass on to you in conclusion, from Paul Meyer: "The man who expects great things, makes noble plans and daily pursues them, cannot help but succeed." And here's the other one: "Whatever we vividly imagine, ardently desire, sincerely believe in, and enthusiastically act upon must inevitably come to pass." Notice the progressive action in these statements. Nothing great is ever attained overnight. But once we set a great goal and commit ourselves toward the achievement of that goal, we have really then just begun to live. Life then takes on dramatic new meaning. You can cultivate the habit of succeeding.

Your Success Checkup

1. What are the four reasons Vernon Howard gives for effective relaxation?
2. State the four categories of people who miss sleep, by Dr. Herman Jahr.
3. Restate the five-point formula for sleeping better.
4. Elmer Wheeler gives us eleven statements on ways to sleep better. List them.
5. Review the twenty-point formula for being well-adjusted as stated by Earl Nightingale.
6. What are the ten rules for overcoming fear?
7. What is Dr. Maxwell Maltz' formula on "How to Achieve Success"?

BIBLIOGRAPHY

Baker, Samm, *Your Key to Creative Thinking* (New York: Harper and Row, 1962).

Bennett, Arnold, *How to Live on Twenty-four Hours a Day* (New York: Doubleday, 1934).

Bettger, Frank, *Benjamin Franklin's Secret of Success* (Englewood Cliffs, New Jersey: Prentice-Hall, Inc., 1960).

——————, *How I Multiplied My Income and Happiness in Selling* (Englewood Cliffs, New Jersey: Prentice-Hall, Inc., 1954).

——————, *How I Raised Myself From Failure to Success in Selling* (Englewood Cliffs, New Jersey: Prentice-Hall, Inc., 1958).

Bogardus, Emory, *Leaders and Leadership* (New York: Appleton-Century-Crofts, 1934).

Bristol, Claude, *Magic of Believing* (Englewood Cliffs, New Jersey: Prentice-Hall, Inc., 1948).

Bristol, Claude and Sherman, Harold, *TNT, The Power Within You* (Englewood Cliffs, New Jersey: Prentice-Hall, Inc., 1954).

Carel, Alexis, *Man, the Unknown* (New York: MacFadden, 1961).

Carnegie, Dorothy, ed., *Dale Carnegie's Scrapbook* (New York: Simon and Schuster, 1959).

Cerami, Charles, *Successful Leadership in Business* (Englewood Cliffs, New Jersey: Prentice-Hall, Inc., 1955).

Chase, JoAnne and Moon, Constance, *You Can Change Your Life Through Psychic Power* (New York: Pocket Books, Inc.).

Churchill, Winston, ed. F. B. Czarnomski, *The Eloquence of Winston Churchill* (New York: Signett, 1957).

Clark, Marguerite, *Why So Tired?* (Greenwich, Conn.: Crest Books, 1962).

Cowles, Edward Spencer, *Don't Be Afraid* (New York: Wilcox and Follett, 1941).

Davidson, Clinton, *How I Discovered the Secret of Success in the Bible* (Westwood, New Jersey: Fleming H. Revell Co., 1961).

Dressler, Marie, *My Own Story* (Boston: Little, Brown, Inc., 1934).

Dumont, Theron Q., *The Power of Concentration* (New York: Wehman Brothers Publishers, 1918).

Eavey, C. B., *The Principles of Mental Health for Christian Living* (Chicago: Moody Press).

Edwards, Tyron, *The New Dictionary of Thoughts* (New York: Standard Book Co., 1955).

Ewing, D. H., *The Harvard Business Review* (September, 1964).

Fink, David Harold, *Release From Nervous Tension* (New York: Simon and Schuster, 1943).

Gore, Michael, *How to Organize Your Time* (New York: Doubleday, 1959).

Haddock, Frank, *Power of the Will* (Cleveland: Ralston Publishing Co., 1948).

Hill, Napoleon, *How to Sell Your Way Through Life* (Cleveland: Ralston Publishing Co., 1958).

——————, *The Law of Success* (Cleveland: Ralston Publishing Co., 1965).

——————, *The Master Key to Riches* (Greenwich, Conn.: Fawcett Publications, Inc.).

Hocking, William, *Types of Philosophy* (New York: Charles Scribner's Sons, 1960).

Hoffer, Eric, *The True Believer* (New York: Harper & Brothers, 1951).

Howard, Vernon, *Action Power* (Englewood Cliffs, New Jersey: Prentice-Hall Inc., 1963).

——————, *Success Through the Magic of Personal Power* (Englewood Cliffs, New Jersey: Prentice-Hall Inc., 1961).

Kingdom, Frank, *How to Strengthen Your Will Power* (New York: Doubleday, 1956).

Laird, Donald A. and Eleanor C., *Tired Feelings and How to Master Them* (New York: McGraw-Hill, 1960).

Levenstein, Aaron, *Why People Work* (New York: Crowell-Collier, 1964).

Liebman, Joshua, *Peace of Mind* (New York: Simon and Schuster, 1946).

Lincoln, James F., *Incentive Management* (Cleveland: Lincoln Electric Co., 1951).

Lindgren, Henry Clay, *How to Live With Yourself and Like It* (Greenwich, Conn.: Fawcett).

Maltz, Maxwell, *The Magic Power of Self-Image Psychology* (Englewood Cliffs, New Jersey: Prentice-Hall, Inc., 1964).

Martin, Clement G., *How to Live to Be 100* (New York: Frederick Fell, 1963).

Milt, H. and Stevenson, G., *Master Your Tensions and Enjoy Living Again* (Englewood Cliffs, New Jersey: Prentice-Hall, Inc., 1959).

Murphy, Joseph, *The Power of Your Subconscious Mind* (Englewood Cliffs, New Jersey: Prentice-Hall, Inc., 1963).

Peale, Norman Vincent, *The Amazing Results of Positive Thinking* (Englewood Cliffs, New Jersey: Prentice-Hall, Inc., 1959).

Ray, Marie, *How Never to Be Tired* (Indianapolis: Bobbs-Merrill, 1938).

Schindler, John A., *How to Live 365 Days a Year* (Englewood Cliffs, New Jersey: Prentice-Hall, Inc., 1955).

Seabury, David, *The Art of Living Without Tension* (New York: Harper, 1958).

Still, Joseph W., "Man's Potential and His Performance," *New York Times Sunday Magazine* (November 24, 1957).

Stone, Clement, *The Success System That Never Fails* (Englewood Cliffs, New Jersey: Prentice-Hall, Inc., 1962).

Sweetland, Ben, *Grow Rich While You Sleep* (Englewood Cliffs, New Jersey: Prentice-Hall, Inc., 1962).

————————, *I Will* (Englewood Cliffs, New Jersey: Prentice-Hall, Inc., 1959).

Updegraff, Robert R., *All the Time You Need* (Englewood Cliffs, New Jersey: Prentice-Hall, Inc., 1958).

von Mises, Ludwig, *The Anti-Capitalistic Mentality* (Princeton, New Jersey: Von Nostrand Co., 1956).

Wheeler, Elmer, *How to Sell Yourself to Others* (Englewood Cliffs, New Jersey: Prentice-Hall, Inc., 1948).

————————, *How to Tap Your Hidden Sources of Energy* (Englewood Cliffs, New Jersey: Prentice-Hall, Inc., 1962).

Williams, J. K., *The Knack of Using Your Subconscious Mind* (Englewood Cliffs, New Jersey: Prentice-Hall, Inc., 1952).

RECORDS

Meyer, Paul J., *How to Master Time Organization* (Success Motivation Institute, 1964).